/ Social Mindscapes

Social Mindscapes

An Invitation to Cognitive Sociology

/

/

/

Eviatar Zerubavel

Harvard University Press
Cambridge, Massachusetts
London, England

First Harvard University Press paperback edition, 1999

Library of Congress Cataloging-in-Publication Data
Zerubavel, Eviatar.
    Social mindscapes : an invitation to cognitive sociology / Eviatar
Zerubavel.
        p.   cm.
    Includes bibliographical references and index.
    ISBN 0-674-81391-X (cloth)
    ISBN 0-674-81390-1 (pbk.)
    1. Social perception.   2. Knowledge, Sociology of.   I. Title.
BF323.S63Z47   1997
302'.1—dc21   97-22037

This book has been digitally reprinted. The content remains identical to
that of previous printings.

To my father,
my first cognitive guide

/ Preface

My interest in studying cognition goes back to 1970, when I first read about human perception in a social psychology class in college. Though immediately fascinated by the topic, I was initially discouraged by my belief that it was not something that I would ever be able to study as a sociologist. The possibility of integrating my interests in the social and the mental became somewhat clearer a year later, when I read Karl Mannheim's *Ideology and Utopia* and Peter Berger and Thomas Luckmann's *The Social Construction of Reality* and discovered the existence of a "sociology of knowledge." Yet it was not until I came to the University of Pennsylvania the following year to study with Erving Goffman, who was about to complete *Frame Analysis*, that I got my first close look at what a sociology of thinking might look like.

As a researcher, I first approached the mind through my work in the sociology of time on social frameworks of temporal reference, the temporal differentiation of the sacred from the profane, and the role of calendars in collective memory. At the same time, as a teacher, I found myself launching a far more ambitious project of trying to develop a general sociological framework for dealing with cognitive matters. In 1980 I introduced for the first time (at the University of Pittsburgh) a course titled "Cognitive Sociology," with which I have kept experimenting ever since then at Columbia University, the State University of New York at Stony Brook, and for the last eight years at Rutgers University. Only in 1987, however, did I begin to seriously consider writing a comprehensive introduction to this field, and only in 1993 did I finally decide to do so, a decision greatly inspired by some encouraging suggestions from both Sherry Turkle and my soon-to-be-editor Michael Aronson.

A number of people deserve an acknowledgment of appreciation for their considerable efforts in helping me make this book better than it would have been without them. I owe special thanks to my colleagues Karen Cerulo and Richard Williams as well as to my students Lisa Bonchek, Wayne Brekhus, Johanna Foster, and Ruth Simpson for taking the time to read and give me some very useful comments on an early draft of the manuscript. I also benefited tremendously from extensive feedback I got from my former student Christena Nippert-Eng, whose own *Home and Work* is an excellent example of a successful attempt to produce a cognitive sociology of everyday life.

Three colleagues and friends deserve a special acknowledgment for the great help they offered me as I was writing this book. Murray Davis, a true intellectual soulmate, is one of the very few fellow travelers I have met over the past twenty years in the rather lonely world of the sociology of the mind, and his excellent feedback on the manuscript was particularly helpful. Kathleen Gerson has shared many of my ups and downs while working on the book, and her extremely careful reading of the manuscript was a rare token of friendship as well as an author's dream come true. As one of the very few sociologists who appreciate the need to bring sociology and cognitive science closer together, Paul DiMaggio was a third ideal reader, and his comments on the manuscript were the most extensive intellectual feedback I have ever received.

A final word of deep appreciation and gratitude to my wife and friend-for-life, Yael, for the excellent feedback she has given me throughout the three years of working on this book. More important, she has continuously provided me with personal and intellectual encouragement and support for the twenty-three years of preparing for it. I shall always treasure her unfailing faith in me throughout this time.

/ Contents

It is not men in general who think, or even isolated individuals who do the thinking, but men in certain groups who have developed a particular style of thought ... Strictly speaking it is incorrect to say that the single individual thinks. Rather it is more correct to insist that he participates in thinking further what other men have thought before him.

Karl Mannheim, *Ideology and Utopia*

1 /

The Sociology of
the Mind

Why do we eat sardines yet never goldfish, ducks yet never parrots? Why does adding cheese make a hamburger a "cheeseburger" whereas adding ketchup does not make it a "ketchupburger"?[1] And why are Frenchmen less likely than Americans to find snails revolting? By the same token, how do we come to regard gold as more precious than water? How do we figure out which of the things that are said at a meeting ought to be included in the minutes and which ones are to be considered "off the record" and officially ignored? And how do we come to "remember" things that happened long before we were born?

In its present state, cognitive science cannot provide answers to any of these questions. In order to even address them, we may very well need an altogether new vision of "the mind."

When we think about thinking, we usually envision an individual thinker—a chess player analyzing his opponent's last move, a scientist designing an experiment, an old man reminiscing about his childhood, a young girl trying to solve a mathematical problem. This vision, so powerfully captured by Auguste Rodin in his statue *The Thinker,* is a typical product of modern Western civilization, which practically invented individualism. Since the late seventeenth century, it has been bolstered by the "empiricist" theories of knowledge developed by the British philosophers John Locke and George Berkeley, who posited a blank mind, a *tabula rasa*, upon which the world impresses itself through our senses.

Yet while *cognitive individualism*[2] still dominates the popular vision of thinking, modern scholarship strongly rejects such a highly personalized view of the mind. Aside from some small pockets of individualistic resistance in philosophy, economics, and psychoanalysis, few students of the mind today base their general vision of thinking on the image of a solitary thinker whose thoughts are a product of his or her own unique personal experience and idiosyncratic outlook on the world. In fact, if scientists were to study idiosyncratic thought patterns that apply only to particular individuals, we probably would not even consider their findings "scientific."

The rise of modern cognitive science[3] coincides with the decline of the Romantic vision of the individual thinker and a growing interest in the non-personal foundations of our thinking. Inspired by René Descartes's and Immanuel Kant's "rationalist" visions of innate mental faculties that precede our sensory experience of the world and even condition the way we actually organize it in our heads, most cognitive scientists today reject Locke's and Berkeley's visions of an a priori empty mind.[4] The move away from empiricism toward rationalism has placed reason instead of experience at the heart of the process we call "thinking." More important, however, it has also meant substituting the human for the individual as the primary locus of cognition.

It is hard not to notice the dramatic shift of attention from the idiosyncratic to the universal in the modern study of the mind. It is our cognitive commonality as human beings, rather than our uniqueness as individual thinkers, that is at the center of the study of cognition today, and modern theories of the mind typically play down our cognitive idiosyncrasies, highlighting instead what we share in common. As evident from the fact that the theoretical agendas of Noam Chomsky and Jean Piaget still dominate much of modern linguistics and developmental psychology, this trend is most visibly epitomized in the current interest in the common constitution of our verbal apparatus as well as the seemingly universal process of our cognitive development.

Cognitive universalism is clearly the dominant vision of the mind in modern cognitive science, much of which revolves around the search for the universal foundations of human cognition. Even psychologists, philosophers, linguists, and students of artificial intelligence who do not study the brain itself nonetheless claim to explore the way humans think. As evident from their general indifference to their research subjects' biographical background, most cognitive scientists today assume a universal, *human* mind.

It is certainly such universalistic sensitivity that allows cognitive scientists to unravel the universal foundations of human cognition. It is precisely their concern with our cognitive commonality that has helped neuroscientists, psychologists, linguists, and students of artificial intelligence to discover universal patterns in the way we form concepts, process information, activate mental "schemas," make decisions, solve problems, generate meaningful sentences from "deep" syntactic structures, access our memory, and move through the various stages of our cognitive development. Yet it is precisely this commitment to cognitive universalism that is also responsible for what is probably cognitive science's most serious limitation. While it certainly helps cognitive scientists produce a remarkably detailed picture of how we are cognitively "hard wired," it also prevents them from addressing the unmistakably non-universal mental "software" we use when we think.

Thus, their almost exclusive concern with our cognitive commonality *as human beings* prevents cognitive scientists from even addressing major cognitive differences that do not result from any fundamental biological differences such as those between normal adults and children, the brain damaged, the senile, or the mentally retarded. This presents the modern science of the mind with a very serious problem since, unlike the way we typically contrast human and animal (or adult and infant) cognition, we certainly cannot attribute the difference between the ancient Roman and present-day Italian visions of the universe (or between the ways liberals and conservatives view art), for example, to any major difference in their genetic makeup or the physiology of their brains.

It is hardly surprising, therefore, that some rather critical aspects of our thinking are still largely ignored by cognitive science. After all, with the exception of cultural anthropologists and cross-cultural psychologists, most modern students of the mind tend to ignore differences in the way we think—differences not only among individuals but also among different cultures, social groups, and historical periods. As a result, few cognitive scientists today would even consider addressing, for example, the difference between the ways in which gender is conceptualized in California and in Yemen, in which Catholics and Buddhists (or peasants and academics) envision God, or in which most Europeans viewed disease in the early thirteenth century and today. Nor, for that matter, can they help us understand why we reckon time in terms of hours and weeks and associate doves with peace. Such intellectual blind spots certainly leave us with less than a truly comprehensive science of the mind.

When my daughter was six, we had our first talk about what she should do if anyone ever tried to abduct her. The very next morning she proudly recounted to me a dream she had that night about precisely such an attempt, which in fact failed because she managed to apply the skills I had taught her only the day before. Wasn't she lucky, she added, that she happened to learn those skills just hours before she needed to use them for the first time! I have told this story to many people and discovered that they almost all find it amusing. Yet there was nothing inherently funny about my daughter's remark. In fact, very few people, if any, would have considered it funny only a hundred years ago, prior to the publication of Sigmund Freud's *The Interpretation of Dreams,*[5] which totally transformed the way we think about our dreams.

At the same time, however, while this should certainly remind us that the things we find amusing are not inherently (and therefore universally) funny, we should also recognize that what we are seeing here are more than just a bunch of unrelated individuals with some peculiar sense of humor that somehow happens to be shared by most of their contemporaries yet, for some odd reason, by no one older than their grandparents. In a similar vein, when we notice that many Americans find the idea of eating snails revolting, we should recognize that what we are seeing is more than just a random collection of individuals with some peculiar phobia that somehow happens to be shared by so many of their compatriots yet, for some odd reason, by only a few French.

The problem with cognitive science is that, except for work produced by cultural psychologists, cognitive anthropologists, and lately some developmental and social psychologists, it has thus far largely ignored the social dimension of cognition. A truly comprehensive science of the mind must also include a *sociology of thinking*[6] that, by focusing specifically on the *sociomental*,[7] would complement the efforts of psychology, linguistics, the neurosciences, and artificial intelligence to provide a complete picture of how we think.

Despite a long history of almost totally ignoring sociology, cognitive scientists need to be more open to what *cognitive sociology*[8] can offer them. Like the other cognitive sciences, it certainly tries to stay away from our cognitive idiosyncrasies, yet whereas psychology or linguistics dwell almost exclusively on our cognitive commonality as human beings, cognitive sociology also highlights major differences in the way we think. In other words, it tries to explain why our thinking is *similar to as well as different from* the way other people think.

There are three rather distinct levels of analysis one can use for approaching cognition given the fact that we think both (a) as individuals, (b) as social beings, and (c) as human beings. Whereas cognitive individualism naturally addresses only the first of those three levels, cognitive universalism basically confines itself to the third. Each, therefore, is somewhat limited in its scope. In addressing the middle level, which covers the entire range between thinking as an individual and as a human being (thereby including, for example, thinking as a lawyer, as a German, as a baby boomer, as a Catholic, and as a radical feminist), cognitive sociology thus helps avoid the reductionistic tendencies often associated with either of those two extremes.

Only an integrative approach that addresses *all* three levels, of course, can provide a complete picture of how we think.[9] While cognitive individualism may certainly shed light on the particular mnemonic techniques I use to remember the password to my electronic mail account and cognitive universalism may best explain how I generally store information in my brain, only a *sociology* of memory can possibly account for how I remember the Crimean War. By the same token, whereas in order to understand how we differentiate "figures" from their surrounding "ground" we clearly need a psychology of perception, only a *sociology* of perception can account for a culture's general tendency to perceive children as resembling their mothers more than their fathers.

In highlighting the social aspects of cognition, cognitive sociology reminds us that we think not only as individuals and as human beings, but also as social beings, products of particular social environments that affect as well as constrain the way we cognitively interact with the world.[10] In probing the social underpinnings of the mental, it thus brings to the foreground a largely neglected dimension of our thinking, the full implications of which cognitive science has yet to explicitly address. As such, it should certainly be an indispensable component of a truly comprehensive science of the mind.

Drawing upon a long sociological tradition most illustriously represented by Emile Durkheim, Karl Mannheim, George Herbert Mead, and Alfred Schutz, cognitive sociology recognizes the fact that we do not think just as individuals. Like the other cognitive sciences, it strongly rejects the extreme individualistic vision of the absolutely original solitary thinker, reminding me, for example, that it is not as an individual but as a product of a particular social environment that I dismiss the fundamentalist account of the current AIDS epidemic as sheer nonsense, and that if my ten-year-old son already knows that the earth is round and that the world is made up of atoms it is only because he happens to live in the twentieth century. It also helps remind me that the way I think about death, God, or sex, for example, is remarkably similar to the way so many other twentieth-century Westerners happen to think about those matters.

Recognizing our cognitive commonality entails rejecting the Romantic vision of some "mental Robinson Crusoe" and remembering that even Crusoe, though far from any other Europeans, was actually still thinking and acting in an unmistakably eighteenth-century British manner. It also entails abandoning Locke's and Berkeley's cognitive empiricism and realizing that perceiving works of art as "Postimpressionist" or "primitive" has very little to do with our senses and everything to do with the impersonal, social categories into which we typically force our personal experience. Furthermore, it means noticing that we also think about a lot of things that we have not experienced personally. Engraved in my mind are not only sensory impressions of the letters I now see on my computer screen and the sound of my printer, but also the ideas of Darwin and Rousseau, whom I will never meet, as well as memories of the voyages of Columbus and Verrazano, which took place more than four hundred years before I was born. In short, I experience the world not only personally, through my own senses, but also *impersonally*, through my mental membership in various social communities.

Most of this, of course, attests to the ubiquitous role of language in our lives. Whereas perception alone would inevitably confine me to a strictly sensory experience of the world, language allows me to process reality conceptually and thereby also bypass my senses. In marked contrast to the absolutely personal nature of sensory perception, language is highly impersonal.[11] When I use words such as "loyalty," "arrogance," "authentic," or "alienated," for example, I am using unmistakably social ideas which clearly did not originate in my own mind. As Karl Mannheim put it, it is not "isolated individuals who do the thinking, but men in certain groups who have developed a particular style of thought . . . Strictly speaking it is incorrect to say that the single individual thinks. Rather it is more correct to insist that he participates in thinking further what other men have thought before him."[12]

Indeed, the impersonal nature of language enables us to transcend our subjectivity and communicate with others.[13] Whereas my senses confine me to my own personal experience, language allows me to convey my thoughts to others as well as to share theirs. It is precisely the impersonal nature of language, therefore, that allows any true "meeting of the minds."

The transcendence of subjectivity and the social construction of *intersubjectivity*[14] help define the distinctive scope and focus of the sociology of the mind. Essentially rejecting cognitive individualism, cognitive sociology ignores the inner, personal world of individuals, basically confining itself to the impersonal social mindscapes we *share in common*.[15]

Such "mindscapes," however, are by no means universal. What we cognitively share in common we do not only as human beings but also as social beings—as Hungarians, as vegetarians, as photographers, as Methodists.

As we try to avoid the strictly personal, we need to be careful not to equate the impersonal with the universal. In other words, when rejecting cognitive individualism, we need not go all the way to the other extreme and replace it by cognitive universalism. While some aspects of our thinking are indeed either purely personal or absolutely universal, many others are neither.

Approaching cognition from an intermediate perspective that complements yet avoids the extremist stances offered by cognitive individualism and universalism, cognitive sociology keeps reminding us that while we certainly think both as individuals and as human beings, what goes on inside our heads is also affected by the particular *thought communities*[16] to which we happen to belong. Such communities—churches, professions, political movements, generations, nations—are clearly larger than the individual yet considerably smaller than the entire human race. The fact that many of the "mindscapes" we commonly share are not universal also implies that they are neither naturally nor logically inevitable. Indeed, they are quite often utterly *conventional*.

As we try to stay away from the strictly subjective, we need not go all the way to the other extreme and regard everything that is not subjective as therefore necessarily objective. Indeed, we should try to avoid the dangerous epistemological pitfall of reification[17] and refrain from attributing absoluteness and inevitability to what is actually merely conventional. While much of our thinking indeed transcends our subjectivity, it is nevertheless often grounded in our common social experience and not just in our "human nature" or some absolute standard of "reason."[18] After all, it is not naturally inevitable to associate owls with wisdom or to mentally relegate waiters in cocktail parties to the "background." Nor, for that matter, is the common distinction we make between violence on the street and on the football field an inherently "logical" one.

Cognitive sociology helps us avoid the danger of regarding the merely conventional as if it were part of the natural order by specifically highlighting that which is not entirely subjective yet at the same time not entirely objective either. Between the purely subjective inner world of the individual and the absolutely objective physical world "out there" lies an intersubjective, social world that is quite distinct from both of them.[19] Unlike the former, it certainly transcends our subjectivity and can therefore be commonly shared by entire thought communities. At the same time, in marked contrast to the latter, it is neither naturally nor logically inevitable.

This intersubjective, social world is quite distinct from the subjective world of the individual as well as from the objective world of nature and logic. It is a world where time is reckoned according to neither the sun or the moon nor our own inner sense of duration but, rather, in accordance with standard, conventional time-reckoning systems such as clock time and the calendar. It is a world where the conventional categories into which we force different "types" of books, films, and music are based on neither our own personal sensations nor any objective logical necessity. Such a world, of course, constitutes the distinctive domain of the sociology of the mind.

The epistemological effort to refrain from attributing objectivity to that which is only intersubjective has some important methodological implications. Since the social world is regarded as natural only by those who happen to inhabit it and therefore take it for granted, the more we can gain access to social worlds that are different from the one we have come to regard as a given the more we will be able to recognize the social nature of both.

Thus, in marked contrast to the tendency among most psychologists, philosophers, linguists, and neuroscientists today to focus on our cognitive commonality as human beings, cognitive sociology tries to promote greater awareness of our *cognitive diversity* as social beings. The more we become aware of our *cognitive differences* as members of different thought communities, the less likely we are to follow the common ethnocentric tendency to regard the particular way in which we ourselves happen to process the world in our minds as based on some absolute standard of "logic" or "reason" and, thus, as naturally or logically inevitable.

Just as it resists the Romantic appeal of cognitive individualism by calling attention to the remarkably similar manner in which different individuals actually classify the world, focus their attention, or reckon time, cognitive sociology also challenges the "imperialistic" claims of cognitive universalism by highlighting major differences in the way members of different thought communities perform those mental acts—differences that clearly cannot be attributed only to their cognitive idiosyncrasies as individuals. Its main goal is to show that our cognitive habits are not so different as to be utterly idiosyncratic yet at the same time also not so similar as to be absolutely universal.

Hence the need for a *comparative* approach to cognition[20] that would highlight our cognitive diversity as members of different thought communities. Such an approach should contrast the cognitive habits of Austrians and Indonesians, Mormons and Muslims, surgeons and sculptors, college graduates and high-school dropouts in a conscious effort to rid us of the common illusion that we think only as individuals and as human beings.

The clearest evidence of our cognitive diversity as members of different thought communities, of course, is the existence of numerous culturally specific *cognitive traditions*. The striking contrast between traditional Gypsy and Eskimo styles of mental delineation, for example,[21] certainly reminds us that there is more than just a single natural or "logical" way of classifying the world. Notable differences between Western and Navajo styles of propositional reasoning[22] are likewise indicative of our considerable cognitive diversity as members of different cultures.

Drawing on a long philosophical, psychological, and anthropological tradition associated with figures like Johann Gottfried Herder, Wilhelm Wundt, and Benjamin Lee Whorf,[23] cognitive sociology indeed views culture as a major locus of cognition. Furthermore, following in the intellectual footsteps of cultural psychology, it goes beyond even cognitive anthropology in its explicit commitment to a comparative, cross-cultural perspective on cognition.[24]

Furthermore, in its commitment to examine cognition from a comparative perspective, cognitive sociology also goes beyond cultural psychology in identifying significant non-idiosyncratic cognitive differences within the same culture. Most spectacular, in this regard, are intracultural historical changes in cognition, such as the declining role of religion in French clinical and legal reasoning over the past few centuries or subtle shifts in Americans' attention to individuals' sex, age, and race over the past few decades.[25] Indeed, the waxing and waning of both cognitive individualism and cognitive universalism over the last three hundred years suggests that whether we associate thinking with individuals or with human beings is in itself affected by various social changes in our intellectual climate. Yet generation-specific cognitive traditions are only one particular instance of the considerable cognitive diversity that exists among different social groups even within the same culture. Consider the profound differences between the way astronomers and mystics envision the universe, for example, or between lawyers' and social workers' general traditions of mental focusing. Indeed, identifying the various *cognitive subcultures* that exist within a given society is one of the most important tasks of cognitive sociology.[26]

Its particular sensitivity to non-idiosyncratic cognitive differences also leads the sociology of the mind to focus on social discord over cognitive matters. The fact that the very definition of justice, art, or obscenity, for example, is often contested even within the same society helps remind us that the way we happen to organize the world in our minds is neither naturally nor logically inevitable. Just as instructive, in this regard, are *cognitive battles* over contested memories. Such battles are typically between social "camps" rather than simply between individuals, of course, suggesting that they are more than just personal. At the same time, the fact that they even exist helps remind us that the way we happen to process reality in our own minds is by no means universal.

Another striking cognitive difference specifically addressed by the sociology of the mind is the one between ordinary, "normal" thinkers and *cognitive deviants* such as the demented, whom we typically regard as "mentally disturbed" because they focus their attention, frame their experience, classify the world, reckon the time, and reason somewhat differently from the rest of us.[27] The existence of cognitive deviance reminds us once again that the way most of us happen to process the world in our minds is neither naturally nor logically inevitable. It also implies the existence of various *cognitive norms*[28] that affect as well as constrain the way we think.

Thus, it is social rules of focusing, for example, that lead us to disregard certain aspects of our surroundings as mere "background." By the same token, social rules of remembrance tell us what we should remember and what we may (or even must) forget. Various conventional rules of mental association likewise affect the meaning we come to attribute to things.

Mental acts such as perceiving, attending, and remembering are not just physiologically constrained human acts but also unmistakably social acts bound by specific normative constraints. Ignoring or forgetting something thus often presupposes some social pressure, however tacit, to exclude it from our attention or memory.

Thinking, in short, has an important normative dimension that has thus far been largely ignored by students of the mind yet which cognitive sociology specifically addresses. It is society, after all, that determines what we come to regard as "reasonable" or "nonsensical," and it usually does so by exerting tacit pressure which we rarely even notice unless we try to resist it.[29] As a result of such pressure, I come to perceive sounds I hear as "classical" or "popular" and to reckon the time in standard, conventional terms such as "8:32," "Wednesday," "February," and "1995" even when I am all by myself.

Like any other social norm, cognitive norms are something we learn. In other words, we *learn* how to focus our attention, frame our experience, generalize, and reason in a socially appropriate manner.

We likewise learn to see things as similar to or different from one another. After all, whenever we classify things, we always regard only some of the differences among them as significant and ignore others as negligible and therefore irrelevant,[30] yet which differences are considered significant is something we learn, and ignoring those that "make no difference" involves tacit social pressure to disregard them despite the fact that we do notice them, just as we learn that in order to find a book in a bookstore we must attend to the first letters of its author's last name while ignoring the color of its cover. Separating the relevant from the irrelevant, as we shall see, is not just a logical but also a normative matter. We likewise learn to "see" the fine lines separating liberals from conservatives and the edible from the inedible. Like the contours of our celestial constellations, we notice such lines only after we learn that we should expect to find them there! In the same way, we also learn to ignore the moral plight of cockroaches and remember the Crusades.

This brings us to another major cognitive difference of critical importance to the sociology of the mind, namely the difference between children and adults. Unlike adults, young children do not "see" the fine lines separating Serbs from Croats, the normal from the perverse, or the sacred from the profane. As evident from the way they experience Santa Claus or the Tooth Fairy,[31] nor do they notice the conventional mental fences separating the "real" world from the worlds of fiction, fantasy, and play. When my son was three and pretended that he was an eagle, he believed that his eagleness was evident not only to the other children who were playing with him but to all the birds around them as well.

Young children who have not learned yet how to focus their attention in a socially appropriate manner and therefore attend to that which is supposed to be disregarded likewise remind us that ignoring the irrelevant is something we learn to do (like my friend's son, who, on his first visit to the zoo, instead of looking at the animals, kept focusing on the patterns in the chain-link fence surrounding the areas where they were kept).[32] A three-year-old boy attending a circus show for the first time cannot "see" the fine line that, to the adults around him, so clearly separates the elephant trainers "in the spotlight" from the attendants who clean after them "in the background." Neither can a three-year-old girl attending her first track meet comprehend why "practice" efforts produced by long jumpers and shot putters are not even measured. Nor, for that matter, can two-year-olds play chess or participate in a real conversation, as they have yet to acquire the ability to jointly share a common focus of attention with others.[33]

Yet the difference between children's and adults' cognition has to do with the fact that they are at rather different stages of their cognitive development not only as human beings but also as social beings. Learning to reckon the time in terms of "seven-thirty," "Wednesday," or "July," for example, is part of the process of becoming social that has nothing to do with our psychocognitive development and everything to do with our *sociocognitive development*.[34] That is also true of the process of learning to distinguish the noble from the crude, ignore the "empty" spaces between buildings,[35] regard gerbils as pets and mice as pests, use Peter Pan, Robinson Crusoe, and Cinderella as metaphors, and remember Moses, Galileo, and Attila the Hun.

As even developmental psychologists are beginning to recognize (mainly as a result of the growing influence of Lev Vygotsky's radical critique of the classic Piagetian view of how we mentally develop),[36] our cognitive development is always situated within a particular social context and constrained by specific social circumstances.[37] Rather than a solitary individual developing in a vaccum, the child is essentially a cognitive "apprentice," socially instructed by others.[38]

It is the process of *cognitive socialization* that allows us to enter the social, intersubjective world. Becoming social implies learning not only how to act but also how to think in a social manner. As we become socialized and learn to see the world through the mental lenses of particular thought communities, we come to assign to objects the same meaning that they have for others around us, to both ignore and remember the same things that they do, and to laugh at the same things that they find funny. Only then do we actually "enter" the social world.

Some of our cognitive socialization is done quite explicitly through formal education, which accounts for the considerable cognitive differences between people with different amounts of formal schooling (not to mention between the literate and the illiterate) even within the same society.[39] Yet unlike our moral and behavioral socialization (as manifested in our laws and rules of etiquette), much of it is also tacit.[40] When a young boy returns with his mother from a long day downtown and hears her "official" account of what they did and saw there, for example, he is getting a tacit lesson in what is considered relevant (and memorable) and irrelevant (and forgettable). Though it is only implicit, such a lesson is an important part of the process of learning how to attend, as well as how to remember, in a socially appropriate manner.

Consider also the way we learn various conventional distinctions. Such cognitive socialization is sometimes explicit, as when we learn in the classroom the difference between fruits and vegetables or gases and liquids, yet much of it is simply "picked up." By noting that some guests always come to her house as part of a larger group whereas others also come by themselves (or that some of them also eat in her kitchen whereas others eat only in the dining room), a young girl implicitly learns the fine cultural distinctions between formal and informal relations as well as between various degrees of intimacy. In a similar vein, by noting that some things in his apartment are always kept in the bedroom or inside drawers whereas others are conspicuously displayed in the living room or on the wall, a young boy also learns the important social distinction between the private and the public. The presence of special clothes and tableware on holidays likewise helps introduce both of them to the equally elusive cultural distinction between the special and the ordinary.[41]

Such tacit socialization is also an inevitable part of the process of learning a language. After all, when young French speakers learn to address some people as *tu* and others as *vous*, they are being implicitly sensitized to the cultural distinction between formal and informal relations. By the same token, learning that hats are considered grammatically masculine whereas suitcases are regarded as feminine also introduces them to gender distinctions in general.

Furthermore, language helps us "typify" the world and thereby transform every novel experience into a somewhat familiar one.[42] Thus, by downplaying their uniqueness and regarding them as typical members of certain categories, I come to feel that I somehow know what to expect from a "guest" or a fellow "passenger" whom I have never met. Likewise, whenever I go to a "funeral," a "wedding," or a "job interview," I already have a rough idea of what it will be like.

The fact that we undergo massive cognitive socialization underscores the considerable amount of control society has over what we attend to, how we reason, what we remember, and how we interpret our experiences. Since it is normally taken for granted except when we actively try to resist it, such *sociomental control* is one of the most insidious forms of social control.

And yet, people in any given social environment are clearly not all cognitive clones of one another, which suggests that the way we think is by no means determined totally by society. Each of us is a member of more than just one thought community[43] and therefore inhabits several different social worlds.[44] As a result, we each have a rather wide "cognitive repertoire" and often think somewhat differently in different social contexts.

Such cognitive diversity happens to be one of the major features of modern life. Indeed, despite the obvious homogenizing effects of television,[45] advertisement, and popular culture, modern society is characterized by its *cognitive pluralism*.[46]

The roots of modern cognitive pluralism are partly structural. Greater social mobility (as manifested, for example, in considerably higher rates of immigration, intermarriage, and remarriage) inevitably produces modern affiliation patterns that, in marked contrast to the somewhat "monocentric" structure of more traditional social networks,[47] involve membership in more than just a single social community.[48] As a result, most people nowadays belong to multiple thought communities.[49]

To appreciate the cognitive implications of such a distinctively modern "web of sociomental affiliations," consider the social structure of our memories. The modern individual is typically situated at the intersection of several quite separate "mnemonic communities" and there is very little overlap between his or her memories as an American, as a criminal lawyer, and as a *Star Trek* fan. This inevitably diminishes our mnemonic commonality with other individuals. Whereas in a more traditional, "monocentric" social structure individuals' recollections are not that different from those of others (consider, for example, the war memories of different members of the same platoon or submarine), that is rarely the case for most of us today.

This, in fact, may also help explain the considerable appeal and resilience of cognitive individualism. Given that we are socially situated at unique intersections of rather separate thought communities, our cognitive makeup also tends to be unique. As the networks of my social affiliations become more complex, my memories, for example, inevitably become more individuated and, thus, personal. After all, who else besides me also shares the collective memories of such separate mnemonic communities as Rutgers University, the track world, and my wife's family?

Modern cognitive pluralism is also a by-product of the growing structural as well as functional differentiation within modern society. In an increasingly compartmentalized and specialized world, we should not be surprised to also find greater cognitive diversity. As we become both structurally and functionally more different from one another,[50] we also come to inhabit more specialized thought communities.

In every society there is an element of social differentiation that calls for some specialized forms of cognitive socialization. In modern society, however, where the division of labor is particularly complex, there is also a more complex *cognitive division of labor*.[51] After all, one would not expect an art dealer, a cook, and a travel agent to share the same stock of professional knowledge,[52] just as one would not expect the cognitive skills of police detectives to resemble those of baseball players or mechanical engineers. In a world where eye and ear doctors may no longer read the same professional journals, it is hardly surprising that even young children get to choose their own electives at school.

The process of cognitive socialization does not end at the age of six, but continues indefinitely as we keep entering new thought communities. In addition to our basic, "primary" cognitive socialization, where we are inducted into society at large and acquire the knowledge and cognitive skills expected from every single one of its members, we also undergo various forms of "secondary" cognitive socialization, where we acquire the more specialized knowledge and skills that are required in specific sectors within it.[53] As a young child, I thus learn to speak, read, and count—"primary" cognitive skills that are expected from practically everyone else around me (yet which may vary from one society to another as well as historically within a given society). Later, however, I acquire the more specific knowledge expected from a librarian (but not from a dentist), the more specialized vocabulary I will need as a food critic (but not as a stock broker), or the particular style of mental focusing required from surgeons (but not from poets).

Yet the roots of modern cognitive pluralism are partly ideological as well. The modern opposition to any form of intellectual hegemony, for example, is directly responsible for the decline of religion's practically monopolistic authority over individuals' cognitive socialization, which has in turn led to a proliferation of widely different "thought styles" that are at considerable odds with one another.[54] Consider also the distinctively modern rejection of traditionalism, which inevitably reduces our cognitive commonality. After all, in a world where computer software programs are revised almost every other year (in marked contrast to traditional "canonical" texts such as the Vedas or the Bible, which have yet to be fundamentally revised after a couple of millennia), there is clearly less and less that individuals cognitively share in common.

The modern rejection of tradition is also reinforced by our strong commitment to individuality in general and originality in

Cognitive Individualism	*Cognitive Sociology*	*Cognitive Universalism*
Thinking as individuals	Thinking as members of thought communities	Thinking as human beings
Subjectivity Personal experience	Intersubjectivity Conventional cognitive traditions	Objectivity Natural or logical inevitability
Personal cognitive idiosyncrasies	Cultural, historical, and subcultural cognitive differences	Universal cognitive commonalities

Figure 1.1. The scope and agenda of cognitive sociology

particular. In sharp contrast to more traditional (religious, military, juridical) systems of education, where individuals are basically taught and expected to cognitively reproduce what their predecessors have already thought before them (and which are therefore rarely concerned with plagiarism, for example), modern education promotes a pronouncedly skepticist (and thereby inevitably irreverent) spirit of free inquiry.[55] If there was ever a period in human history when individuality and originality were celebrated to such an extent, it is now. People who only five centuries ago would have been burned alive because they refused to think like everyone else around them actually win Nobel laurels today precisely *because* of their unabashed display of unbridled originality.

This book is an invitation to examine the social foundations of our thinking. It is organized around a discussion of six major cognitive acts—perceiving, attending, classifying, assigning meaning, remembering, and reckoning the time—with each of the following six chapters specifically devoted to one of them. Each of these acts, of course, is performed by specific individuals with certain personal cognitive idiosyncrasies. Each of them, at the same time, is also performed by human beings with certain universal cognitive commonalities. Yet each of these six cognitive acts is also performed by social beings who belong to specific thought communities. It is this latter, social dimension of our thinking that I try to capture.

As evident from Figure 1.1, I highlight the distinctive thrust of cognitive sociology by committing myself throughout the book to a supra-personal yet nevertheless sub-universal level of analysis. In other words, in order to integrate the individualistic and universalistic traditions of approaching cognition, we must focus precisely on what they have thus far left almost untouched between them.

Throughout the book, I therefore specifically stay away from cognitive individualism by calling attention to the strikingly similar manner in which different individuals reckon the time or assign meanings to objects as well as to their common memories and rather similar cognitive maps of the world. In other words, I deliberately ignore the strictly personal world of individuals and their cognitive idiosyncrasies and focus exclusively on the impersonal mindscapes they share. At the same time, however, I also stay away from cognitive universalism by calling attention to their cognitive differences as members of different thought communities. I thus focus on different culturally specific patterns of performing a given cognitive act, major historical changes in the way it has been performed within a given culture, as well as different subculturally specific patterns of performing it within a given society. To further underscore the conventional nature of the way in which we focus our attention, frame our experience, or remember things, I likewise examine the *politics of cognition,* calling attention to major disputes surrounding the performance of those acts within a given society. In an effort to highlight the normative dimension of our thinking, I also identify various social rules (of interpreting, focusing, categorizing, associating, and remembering) that constrain our cognition.

The six cognitive acts I examine in this book, of course, do not exhaust the phenomenon we call "thinking."[56] Exploring their social foundations, however, ought to give us at least a general idea of what cognitive sociology has to offer the modern science of the mind.

2 /

Social Optics

A good way to begin exploring the mind would be to examine the actual process by which the world "enters" it in the first place. The first step toward establishing a comprehensive sociology of the mind, therefore, would be to develop a *sociology of perception.*[1]

The way we perceive things is often influenced by the way they are perceived by others around us.[2] Furthermore, we often perceive them in a social manner even when there is no one else around us. Colors, for example, are recognized much more easily when we have distinct names for them and, since languages vary in the way they cut up the color spectrum, people from different cultures often vary in their color perception.[3] Along similar lines, there are considerable differences between cultures and across different levels of education within the same culture in depth perception, in perceptual organization, and in individuals' susceptibility to optical illusions.[4]

Yet perception is more than what experimental psychologists study in their laboratories, since it involves more than just a sensory experience of the world. The meaning of "sensing," "smelling," or "hearing," for example, clearly transcends its literal connotation. Our "outlook" and "taste" likewise transcend our strictly sensory experience of our physical surroundings.

It is particularly important, in this regard, to address the interpretive dimension of perception, since what we experience through our senses is normally "filtered"[5] through various interpretive frameworks. Indeed, separating the act of "pure" physical perception from the mental processing of the sensory information we obtain through it makes very little sense from an epistemological standpoint. As we shall see, our social environment plays a major role in how we actually interpret things. The way we mentally process what we perceive through our senses is to a large extent socially mediated.

Even perception cannot be reduced to purely sensory experience, essentially underscoring the inherent limitations of a strictly empiricist view of cognition. After all, what we see or hear is also affected by our particular cognitive "orientation" prior to the actual act of perceiving. The experience of listening to a piece of music that I know was written by Mozart, for example, is quite different from that of listening to the very same piece without knowing who wrote it.[6] It is their often-different preconceptions that likewise lead different jurors to perceive the very same factual evidence presented to them in court so differently.

Even when I encounter something for the very first time, my mind is hardly a *tabula rasa*. Indeed, I often have some prior expectations, which accounts for such common experiences as disappointment and surprise.[7] Such expectations are based on schematic mental structures that exist in my mind prior to the actual act of perception and which strongly affect the way I process my sensory experience.[8] We often develop a strong cognitive "commitment" to such structures, to the point of actually trying to make what we perceive through our senses fit them instead of the other way around. In order to make sense of novel situations, we thus often try to mentally force them into such pre-existing schemas.[9]

A classic example of the way we perceive novel objects and situations as mental extensions of familiar schemas is the case of the European "discovery" of America in the 1490s, which is distinctly characterized by Columbus's extremely stubborn attempts to force everything he encountered on its shores into the image of the world he had prior to his arrival there. Not only did that image remain virtually untouched by what he actually found on the other side of the Atlantic, it also affected the way he perceived the latter, as evident from his relentless efforts to force this totally unfamiliar new world into the familiar contours of the old. Thus he identified America as "the Indies" and its native inhabitants as "Indians," and though the natives of Cuba told him that it was only an island, he kept insisting that it was actually part of the Asian mainland. Even when he later admitted to himself that the northern shore of South America was not Asia, he nevertheless proceeded to identify it as the Garden of Eden, thereby cosmographically "placing" it in a way that would still not compel him to transgress the confines of his preconceived image of a tricontinental world. Indeed, his prior expectations distorted even his sensory impressions of America, leading him to "hear" the natives of Costa Rica say that he was only a couple of weeks away from the Ganges as well as to "find" in the New World exclusively Old World plants such as cinnamon and nutmeg![10]

The way in which our perception is affected by our prior cognitive orientation is also quite evident in science. Even in the world of natural, "hard" science, what one observes is never totally independent of the particular "lens" through which it is mentally processed. Even seemingly objective scientific "facts," in other words, are affected by the particular mental filters through which scientists process what they observe in their heads. When scientists turn their telescopes or microscopes to the world around them, their minds are not *tabulae rasae* passively waiting to register the sensory impressions they are about to receive. Even astronomers and microbiologists do not simply observe the world "as it is." How they perceive it is always affected by their particular cognitive orientations prior to the actual act of observing it.[11]

Hence the "optical" significance of scientific revolutions. Contrary to popular belief, the main thrust of such revolutions is far more epistemological than strictly factual.[12] They are primarily cognitive upheavals that radically transform the way we "look" at the world. While they may not always involve the discovery of any new facts, they do offer us new *mental lenses* through which old ones may be seen in a new way.

Indeed, it is not always new factual findings that even prompt such revolutions in the first place but, quite often, a reexamination of some old facts (such as the daily rising and setting of the sun in the case of the Copernican revolution in astronomy) through some new mental lenses. In other words, great scientific discoveries are often the result of dramatic epistemological shifts that involve "looking" at the very same reality from an altogether new mental angle. By simply shifting our *mental* gaze, we may thus come to "see" things we have never noticed before, even in extremely familiar environments (like Boggle players who start noticing new words as soon as they change the angle from which they look at the jumbled letters before them).

Consider, for example, the great revolution in modern cosmography prompted by Europe's realization that Columbus was wrong and that America is in fact quite distinct as well as fully detached from Asia. It was certainly not the discovery of some new factual findings that set the early-sixteenth-century Europeans who came to view America as a New World apart from those who, following Columbus, stubbornly maintained that it was only an extension of the Old. (Throughout the sixteenth century, many European cosmographers and cartographers kept insisting that Mexico and China were one and the same and that Asia and North America were actually joined by a land bridge.)[13] When German cosmographer Martin Waldseemüller in 1507 became the first European to explicitly identify America as a new continent fully surrounded by water,[14] it was still six years before Vasco Núñez de Balboa managed to cross the Isthmus of Panama, reach America's western shore, and drive the first nail into Columbus's cosmographic coffin by introducing Europe to the great ocean lying beyond his "Indies."[15] Only in 1778 did James Cook conclusively establish the absolute separateness of North America from northeast Asia.[16] In other words, it took almost three hundred years since Columbus's first encounter with the New World for Europe to have definitive proof that it is indeed fully detached from the Old.

It was not that Waldseemüller had more factual knowledge about the new continent than its official "discoverer." In fact, since he may not have even been to America, he certainly had much less information about it than Columbus, who had actually spent several years there. Rather, it was his readiness to "look" at the newly discovered lands beyond the Atlantic through a new mental lens that led him to figure out that they were both distinct and detached from Asia. Whereas Columbus "viewed" America as a mere extension of the familiar (that is, as a group of islands lying somewhere off the shores of China), Waldseemüller was prepared to re-view it as an altogether new cosmographic entity, and thereby to literally rediscover Columbus's "Indies" as "America."

The shift from regarding America as a mere extension of the Old World to "seeing" it as an altogether separate New World bears a striking resemblance to the historic shift within Western medicine from regarding men and women as merely two variants of a single sex to perceiving them as two entirely distinct sexes—a dramatic cognitive revolution that occurred only relatively recently. Until two centuries ago, Western science basically viewed women not as a distinct sex but as men turned outside in. Human anatomy textbooks thus stressed the structural similarities between the male and female reproductive systems, graphically playing up the considerable morphological affinity between ovaries and testicles or labia and foreskin as well as refraining from assigning various female sexual organs distinct names (and, thus, identities). Only toward the end of the eighteenth century did they start to explicitly call attention to the morphological contrast between men and women, thereby promoting an altogether new "view" of sex.[17]

As with Europe's mental discovery of America, what actually prompted this dramatic change from an essentially isomorphic to a dimorphic view of sex were not any new facts but, rather, a dramatic change in the nature of the mental lenses through which modern medicine has come to view old ones. Our sexual anatomy, after all, did not undergo any radical changes two hundred years ago. Nor were any new factual discoveries made around that time that might have warranted abandoning the traditional isomorphic view of sex. (In fact, modern research in embryology has only further reaffirmed the considerable morphological affinity between males and females.) What did start to change toward the end of the eighteenth century were the social and political relations between men and women in Europe, which led many anxious Europeans to start looking for "hard" evidence of fundamental natural differences between them. The dramatic change in how we have come to view sex, in other words, was prompted not by any changes in our factual knowledge of human anatomy but by major changes in our social and political climate which prompted a strong cognitive need to play up the "obvious" differences, rather than the equally obvious similarities, between women and men.[18]

The history of the Western perception of female genitals reminds us that there is always more than only one way to perceive something. No single "view" of any object, in other words, is inevitable.

Furthermore, the difference between the various views of an object one gets through different mental lenses is not always one between more and less correct ones. It is still not absolutely clear, for example, whether men and women are "indeed" two distinct sexes or just two variants of a single sex. The relation between them is a combination of *both* similarity and difference, and the decision as to which of those one should highlight is therefore by no means inevitable.

At this particular moment in history the dimorphic "view" of sex certainly prevails over the old isomorphic view. Yet just because it happens to be the more recent predominant view does not necessarily mean that it is therefore also the more correct one. Despite the common "contempocentric" tendency to mistake currentness for correctness and thus regard the history of ideas as a linear progression toward some absolute Truth, it is not at all clear why we should assume that our modern vision of sex is indeed objectively more "correct" than its traditional precursor.

One of the important lessons of history is that the mental lenses through which we "see" the world keep changing all the time. As a result, we have no basis for claiming that our own visions of reality are more definitive than were those of our predecessors. Back in the fourteenth century, people were probably just as arrogant about the absolute correctness of their own "view" of the world as we are about ours today.

Even in science (which, more than any other cognitive framework, we tend to regard as a system of absolute truths) there is more than only one mental lens through which one can "observe" things. As a result, there is always more than just a single "scientific" way of perceiving them, and scientists who look at the same reality through different mental lenses indeed often end up generating somewhat different "facts."[19] The difference between different scientific views of reality (such as whether we view light as made of particles or waves, for example) is therefore not always a function of their being more or less factually correct.

This is even more true, of course, of nonscientific (moral, religious, ideological) "views" of the world. Whether a particular painting is to be "seen" as art or sacrilege or whether military dictatorship is to be perceived as a legitimate or a morally unacceptable form of government, for example, cannot ever be objectively resolved. Nor, for that matter, can any of the many disputes between liberals and conservatives over the "correct" way to view taxes, school prayer, intermarriage, or abortion.[20]

"*Optical*" *pluralism* is an inevitable result of the fact that there are many different mental lenses through which one could possibly "see" an object. In other words, there is always more than only one cognitive "standpoint" from which something can be mentally approached. As a result, there is also more than just a single way in which it can be "correctly" perceived. This accounts for our "optical" diversity, the fact that different people often perceive the very same reality somewhat differently.

The way we perceive things is inevitably affected by how we are mentally positioned relative to them (that is, by the particular *perspective* from which we "view" them). And since there is always more than just a single mental stance from which something can be "seen," the same object is very often perceived somewhat differently by different people, as the classic story about the blind men and the elephant so effectively reminds us. After all, the very same magic show certainly looks quite different from the perspectives of young children and adults, and what their clients typically experience as play is usually perceived by prostitutes as work. Tourists' romantic view of an island's sandy beaches is likewise typically lost on the local islanders, who "see" them primarily as the place from which they launch their fishing expeditions every night. That the very same reality may "look" so different to different people is a useful reminder that the particular way in which we happen to perceive something is by no means inevitable. Despite our common tendency to reify it, the particular mental lens through which we look at the world is only one of many possible lenses we could have used.

"Optical" pluralism or "perspectivism" does not preclude the existence of an objective reality. It does, however, tie the validity of the different "views" of that reality to particular standpoints rather than to some absolute Truth.[21] As such, it underscores the inherent futility of any attempt to compare different cognitive outlooks to one another in terms of their "correctness."

The difference between different cognitive "outlooks," in short, is not always one between sharp and blurred vision. Very often, it is a difference between different yet equally valid visions through different mental lenses. It is not unlike the difference between looking at something through a telescope and through a microscope, or between the various angles or distances from which one might look at a painting.[22] After all, there *is* no one correct angle or distance to look at paintings—examining the artist's brush technique and appreciating the picture's overall balance, for example, require altogether different distances, neither of which is necessarily more "correct" than the other. The difference between our various "outlooks" on the world, therefore, is very often a difference between different yet equally valid cognitive alternatives.

Yet the fact that our "interpretive positions"[23] are not inevitable does not mean that they are therefore necessarily all personal and subjective. The schematic mental structures that help us make sense of what we perceive through our senses, for example, are usually based on intersubjective, conventionalized typifications.[24] Society, in short, plays a major role in organizing our "optical" predispositions.[25] Indeed, many of the mental lenses through which we come to "see" the world are actually *socio*mental lenses grounded in particular social environments.

As such, they are also highly impersonal. The particular cognitive standpoint from which I "see" that it is the earth that revolves around the sun rather than the other way around, for example, is also shared by many others around me. When I adopt it, I am thus adopting an unmistakably impersonal outlook that exists independently of me.

Thus, it is not only as individuals but also as members of particular social environments that we become receptive to particular "views" of reality. The mental visions of the world promoted by Darwin, Einstein, Picasso, or Kafka, for example, are generally received today quite differently from the way they probably would have been received eighteen hundred years ago. The difference, however, has little to do with the differences between the personal outlooks of particular second-century and twentieth-century individuals and everything to do with the fundamental difference between the general intellectual climates of those two centuries.[26]

By the same token, it is not only as individuals but also as members of particular social environments that we tend to resist and reject certain "views" of the world. For example, it is not as an individual but as a member of a highly rationalistic, scientifically-minded society that I usually dismiss prophecies made by astrologers and fortune-tellers while at the same time accepting pollsters' and meteorologists' statistically-based predictions and forecasts. It is as a member of a highly secular culture that I likewise tend to dismiss religious accounts of natural disasters as sheer nonsense.

Not only are the cognitive stances we adopt as members of particular social environments external to us, they also constrain our mental "vision" by exerting upon us tremendous pressure to conform to them,[27] which explains the relatively small number of "*optical*" *deviants* who dare to defy or ignore the "*optical*" *norms* of their social environment by maintaining a "view" of the world that is at odds with the one commonly shared by others around them. (The fact that such pockets of deviance nonetheless do exist, however, helps discredit any essentialist approach to perception.) Society may no longer burn such cognitive heretics at the stake, yet they nevertheless still generate scorn and ridicule and even stand the risk of being locked up in mental institutions for having some fundamental "cognitive disorder." There may be potential Freuds and Darwins among us about whom we will never hear only because, unlike Freud or Darwin, they may lack the intellectual courage to voice their heretical views and thereby risk "cognitive excommunication."

"Looking" at the world from an impersonal perspective presupposes a certain cognitive ability to transcend our subjectivity and adopt others' "views" as if they were our own.[28] Such an ability allows us to "see" things not only with our own eyes but also through impersonal mental lenses commonly shared by others around us as general frameworks for organizing their perception.

This presupposes some fundamental process of "*optical*" *socialization* where we learn to "look" at things in unmistakably social ways. After all, children are not born with the conventional mental schemas that later help them make sense of every new situation they encounter. Nor is sociologists' distinctive "view" of the world ("the sociological imagination")[29] something they happen to develop as individuals. Indeed, it is an impersonal outlook which they acquire through their membership in a particular professional community.

"Optical" socialization typically takes place within particular thought communities (a particular profession, a particular religion, a particular generation), which is how we come to perceive things not only as individuals but also as engineers, as Catholics, or as baby boomers.[30] Each of these "optical" communities has its own distinctive "optical" tradition, and membership in it entails learning to "see" the world through its particular mental lenses.

Such "optical" traditions are not just random collections of ways of "seeing" particular objects but, rather, general, global worldviews.[31] The way liberals typically perceive modern art, for example, is not unrelated to their "views" of affirmative action, sex education, or the environment. Nor, for that matter, is conservatives' typical "outlook" on abortion unrelated to the way they view drugs, homosexuality, school prayer, or welfare. Thus, when we talk about conservatism or liberalism, we are actually talking about a general "optical" style[32] of perceiving things.

Such general outlooks typically affect the mental vision of entire "optical" communities and not just particular individuals within them, since they are available to practically everyone who wears the community's distinctive mental lenses and thus commonly shared by all of its members. As such, they are clearly also more than just aggregates of the personal outlooks of all the individual members of the community. In other words, they are genuinely collective.[33]

As a result, within each "optical" community, individuals usually tend to perceive things somewhat similarly, since they basically "see" the world through the same mental lenses. (Indeed, an "optical" community is the social unit from within which the world "looks" the same!) It is, then, a particular society rather than just particular individuals within it that tends to "see" children as resembling their mothers more than their fathers.[34] Similarly, it is the entire profession of landscape design rather than just particular designers that tends to see our physical surroundings primarily in aesthetic terms.

Yet whereas the outlooks of people who belong to the same "optical" community and thus "see" the world through the same mental lenses are basically similar, they are usually quite different from those of people who come from somewhat different social (religious, professional, class) backgrounds and therefore use altogether different ones. While landscape designers may have somewhat similar sensitivities when they see a house, they are considerably different from the ones shared by roofers, firemen, police detectives, or appraisers. By the same token, Ingmar Bergman films "look" quite different to working-class and college-educated audiences, as do nude photographs of women to art students and radical feminists. And the same passage that white readers tend to interpret as involving physical aggression is usually perceived by black readers as rather innocuous.[35] In short, while the world may indeed "look" the same to people who happen to wear the same sociomental lenses, it actually looks quite different to people who do not.

Lest we forget, given our rather intricate webs of social affiliations, each of us is in fact a member of many different "optical" communities. As a result, we often "see" the world somewhat differently as we switch the sociomental lenses through which we actually "view" it. Just as I may perceive the very same person quite differently when I am sexually aroused[36] and when I am not (or a party when I host it or merely attend it as a guest), my perspective on the Holocaust is significantly different when I "look" at it as a sociologist or as a Jew whose father's family was virtually wiped out in it. Having a complete picture of an individual's "web of sociomental affiliations" is therefore critical for understanding the full complexity of how he or she actually "sees" the world.

3 /

The Social Gates of Consciousness

To further appreciate the ubiquitous presence of society in our minds, let us also examine its role in delineating the scope of our attention and concern. As we shall see, not only does our social environment affect how we perceive the world; it also helps determine what actually "enters" our minds in the first place.

Our thinking is inherently limited. There are numerous things about which we could conceivably think yet which nevertheless do not even "cross" our minds. That is true of our purely sensory experience as well. There are many things around us which we could technically perceive through our senses yet which nonetheless remain "outside" our consciousness.

Consider, for example, what we actually see. Not only is our vision inherently bounded by our horizons,[1] our actual visual range is also curbed in the process of *focusing,* where much of what is physically around us is nonetheless excluded from the inner part of our field of vision and relegated to our "peripheral" vision. *Attending* something in a focused manner entails mentally disengaging it (as a "figure") from its surrounding "ground," which we essentially ignore.[2]

Focus, horizon, figure, and ground are all visual images, yet they are also highly evocative metaphors that are extremely useful in analyzing non-visual forms of mental delineation as well.[3] Hence their great value for students of both attention (visual as well as non-visual) and concern.

In an effort to address more than just the more obvious, physical aspects of attention, I shall proceed to examine here the general process of *mental focusing* (as well as the general phenomenon of *mental horizons*). In doing so, I shall likewise expand the traditional meaning of the distinction between "figure" and "ground" to also include the more general distinction between the relevant and the irrelevant, a fundamental distinction that captures the very essence of the process of focusing.

Inevitably, perception also presupposes some *im*perception. After all, in order to be able to perceive the contents of a painting, I must also ignore the wall surrounding it.[4] By the same token, in order to become cognitively sensitized to the ritual aspect of business or to the normative aspect of fashion, sociologists must also become *de*sensitized to their pragmatic and aesthetic aspects first.

As evident from our failure to notice objects which visually blend with their immediate surroundings,[5] mental fusion entails mental dissolution. In order to be able to focus on something, we must perceive some noticeable discontinuity between that which we are to attend and that which we are to ignore. As any active user of camouflage (from rabbits and chameleons to soldiers and cosmeticians) knows, without such discontinuity it is practically impossible to differentiate any mental "figure" from its surrounding ground.

In helping separate the relevant from the irrelevant, it is essentially our mental horizons that enable us to ignore certain parts of reality as mere background and thereby grasp (visually as well as mentally) any "thing" at all. As effective mental limits, they basically protect us from the cognitive predicament of being constantly bombarded by an undifferentiated stream of stimuli. Indeed, it is psychotics' general difficulty with limits that makes it so hard for them to effectively separate the relevant from the irrelevant and thereby attend anything in a focused manner.[6]

Yet delineating our attention also entails some mental constriction. After all, the fine lines that help us separate that which ought to "enter" our minds from everything else inevitably also constrict our thinking. Our mental horizons limit more than just our perceptual field. Like their prototypical exemplars, which literally impose visual closure on our physical surroundings, they basically "close" our minds by helping delineate what we consider relevant. After all, there is much more that could "enter" our consciousness yet is nevertheless excluded as irrelevant because it basically lies "beyond" our mental horizons.

To get a first glimpse of the role of our mental horizons in "closing" our minds, consider some of the things we usually tend to ignore as irrelevant. In an ordinary conversation, rarely do we actually notice the color of the buttons on the shirt of the person with whom we are talking or the kind of watch he is wearing despite the fact that both are clearly within our field of vision. In a business meeting, we usually do not notice who is drinking coffee, adjusting his eyeglasses, or simply doodling. Such "background" activities[7] are normally foregrounded (thereby explicitly forcing themselves into our sphere of focused attention) only when something unusual happens, as when somebody accidentally spills his coffee.

With the possible exception of first dates, psychotherapy sessions, and job interviews, where we tend to regard practically *everything* as relevant, social situations are typically surrounded by mental fences[8] which mark off only part of what is actually included in our perceptual field as relevant, thereby separating that which we are expected to attend in a focused manner from that which we are supposed to leave "in the background" and essentially ignore. Such "frames"[9] are designed to help us disregard a considerable part of our sensory experience as "out-of-frame"[10] and therefore irrelevant.

Consider, for example, the art frame, quintessentially embodied by the picture frame. Picture frames, of course, are specifically designed to help viewers ignore the wall surrounding the picture. In this, they also resemble the mental brackets[11] surrounding concerts, which are supposed to help the audience disregard musicians' "background" activities that are not considered an integral part of the artistic performance in which they are nonetheless visually embedded (replacing a mouthpiece, adjusting one's music stand, wiping the spittle off one's horn).

Consider also the play frame. After all, when we play checkers, the actual material of which the pieces are made is considered irrelevant to the game and therefore out-of-frame. (In fact, when a particular piece happens to be missing, players often replace it with a coin, thereby also disregarding the latter's ordinary monetary value, which is "bracketed off" as irrelevant!) Similarly, when we play chess, we normally ignore mere "accidents" such as unintentionally knocking a piece off the board (not to be confused, of course, with the act of deliberately removing a piece that has been officially captured, which is considered within the play frame and therefore part of the game). In checkers as well as in chess, players' religion, weight, sexual preferences, and political views are likewise bracketed off as absolutely irrelevant to the game.[12]

The mental discontinuity between the framed and the out-of-frame also applies to people. Indeed, it is hard to find a more blatant manifestation of the role of our mental horizons in regulating what actually "enters" our minds than the way we often treat certain people as irrelevant, essentially excluding them from our sphere of attention despite their obvious physical presence within our perceptual field.

As evident from the often-heard question "Who asked *you*, anyway?" mere physical presence at a situation does not necessarily guarantee inclusion in the mental frame surrounding it and delineating what is considered relevant. Very often only some of the people who are actually present at a situation are also considered full-fledged participants in it, whereas others are regarded as mere bystanders who can be practically ignored. These are people who are clearly included within the range of our senses yet who are nonetheless mentally situated out of our focus. (This typically tacit distinction between full-fledged "participants" and mere "bystanders" usually becomes explicit only when the latter, essentially defying their "background" status, unexpectedly force themselves into the former's sphere of attention, as when a kibitzer offers unsolicited advice to cardplayers, or when a nosy cab driver suddenly joins an ongoing conversation among his passengers.)[13]

Nowhere is the way we assign certain people "nonperson"[14] status more blatantly evident than in the case of the very young. It is quite common for adults to not even notice the small children running around them at weddings or picnics (which also accounts for their occasional use, along with housekeepers, butlers, chauffeurs, and other "background people," in various forms of espionage).[15] As a result of their perceived irrelevance, even our ordinary senses of privacy and shame are often suspended in their presence. Thus, for example, it is not uncommon for parents to discuss highly sensitive subjects in front of very young children or even to make love in the presence of infants (thereby practically treating them like lamps, curtains, or chairs).

To get a further glimpse of the role of our mental horizons in "closing" our minds, consider also the process of *moral focusing*. After all, the fine lines separating the relevant from the irrelevant also confine our moral attention to a certain "circle of altruism"[16] which they help delineate. Any object we perceive as lying "outside" this circle (that is, "beyond" our moral horizons) is essentially considered morally irrelevant and, as such, does not even arouse our moral concerns.

Our moral sentiments are rarely ever boundless. After all, even the most inclusive notion of "universalism" nevertheless presupposes some tacitly bounded universe! Even among those who contend that "everyone" in America should have free access to medical care, for example, very few would actually go so far as to extend such moral concerns to also include tourists (not to mention pigeons or raccoons). By the same token, even the strongest advocates of the moral crusade to extend the "basic right to live" to the unborn often refuse to grant the very same right to convicted murderers, who, they believe, have in effect placed themselves beyond society's moral horizons.

Along similar lines, even the most broadly defined notions of altruism (that is, regard for the welfare of others) nevertheless exclude at least some possible objects of concern as morally irrelevant. Most so-called altruists tacitly restrict their definition of "others" to humans, rarely extending it to include the weeds we remove from our lawns, the cockroaches and rats we so casually try to poison, or the dartboards, punching bags, tennis balls, and bowling pins we so brutally attack for fun. Nor, for that matter, do even the most "considerate" among us have much empathy towards the car doors we slam or the candles we burn. And even those who knit little sweaters to protect their puppies from the cold rarely show such concern toward the fish or vegetables lying in their freezers (not to mention the homeless poor).

The mental horizons separating that which actually "enters" our minds from that which is excluded as irrelevant are by no means entirely personal. In other words, when we confine our attention and concern to certain mental tunnels, we do so not just as individuals.

To be sure, individuals do sometimes vary in the way they focus their attention. When people with different interests or concerns read the same newspaper, for example, they often notice different things and regard different things as irrelevant. Nonetheless, the particular way in which we happen to "close" our minds is strikingly similar to the way many others around us close theirs.

Yet the fact that we exclude certain parts of reality from our attention and concern as irrelevant not just as individuals does not necessarily mean that we therefore do so only as human beings. After all, while the particular way in which we happen to "close" our minds is strikingly similar to the way many others around us close theirs, it is also quite different from the way many other humans do, which serves to remind us that our own particular focusing patterns are by no means universal and thereby underscores the need to avoid the common epistemological pitfall of reifying our own horizons and regarding them as inevitable.

Admittedly, the way we differentiate relevant mental "figures" from the irrelevant ground within which they are contextually embedded is partly determined by a number of essentially universal laws of perception.[17] For the most part, however, it is neither naturally nor logically inevitable. Our horizons, in other words, are for the most part neither natural nor logical.

The remarkably similar manner in which building inspectors, for example, happen to focus their professional attention is quite different from similar focusing patterns of polar bears or pelicans, which basically result from certain physiological constraints, just as the difference between the intellectual horizons of economists and theologians is quite different from the difference between the vision ranges of eagles and rhinoceroses or the hearing ranges of cows and gazelles. What members of each of these "optical" communities come to regard as irrelevant and thereby ignore has absolutely nothing to do with any physiological constraints on their ability to perceive the world through their senses.

By the same token, the fine line separating the sounds we consider part of "the concert" from all the other sounds we hear in the concert hall yet somehow try to tune out as irrelevant (muffled coughs, squeaking chairs) is clearly not the result of any physiological constraints on our hearing. Nor, for that matter, is it nature that compels jurors to disregard "inadmissible" evidence presented to them in court or logic that makes exterminators exclude mice and bugs from their sphere of moral concern. Indeed, the fine lines separating that which "enters" our consciousness from that which is considered irrelevant and thereby ignored exist only in our minds. Reality is inherently boundless, and the narrow tunnels to which we normally confine our mental vision are not really part of the world "out there." Forcing essentially open-ended mental fields into neatly bounded "boxes"[18] is but an artificial attempt to introduce some closure into the world.

The very notion of horizons, of course, presupposes closed systems, which, as we all know, one rarely finds in the real world. In other words, we set our own mental horizons and then reify them, like the proverbial ostrich which hides its head in the sand, denying the existence of practically anything that lies beyond its self-imposed horizons. Yet even the narrow-minded ostrich cannot really make everything outside of its own tunnel vision disappear by simply wishing it away. Horizons are mere figments of our minds, and only someone who suffers from total "context blindness"[19] would fail to see that what we manage to mentally push beyond them is not really detached from that which is contained within them. After all, as soon as we turn our necks, our horizons inevitably widen!

Thus, when we exclude certain parts of reality from our attention and concern as irrelevant, we do so not just as human beings but also as social beings. In other words, it is usually as members of particular thought communities that we ignore certain things. It is our social environment that normally determines what we attend and ignore. In helping set the horizons of our attention and concern, it is often society that defines what we consider relevant.

That our mental horizons are for the most part neither natural nor logical is quite evident from the fact that they often vary across cultures. The almost legendary ability of the English to practically disattend others who are clearly within the range of their senses[20] is typically shared by neither Arabs nor Italians. Nor, for that matter, do members of hunting societies and farming societies have the same general capacity to differentiate figures from their visual surroundings.[21]

Consider also the way culture sometimes affects our curiosity. It is quite interesting to note that at the same time that Columbus, Cabot, da Gama, Vespucci, Magellan, Verrazano, and other Western Europeans were exponentially expanding Europe's geographical horizons, the second-largest island of Japan, Hokkaido, was still largely unknown to those who lived on the main island of Honshu just a few miles south of it.[22]

Just as striking, of course, are major cross-cultural differences in moral focusing. Whereas some cultures explicitly stress one's moral responsibility to "think of" the sick, the poor, and the mentally retarded, there are others where at least one of those social categories is considered morally irrelevant. By the same token, while Jain monks in India deliberately avoid vigorous activities such as swimming and digging and carefully dust stools before sitting on them so as not to risk harming even tiny microorganisms,[23] most Westerners do not even consider the use of "pesticides" a moral matter.

Yet patterns of mental focusing also vary across social settings within the same culture, and not everything that we consider relevant in one setting is also considered relevant in others. While few of us even notice whether or not other people around us are chewing gum when we are on the beach or in an amusement park, that very same act would most definitely capture our attention if it were to take place at church or during a job interview. While we typically notice players' height in basketball, we rarely do so in poker.

Furthermore, as I have already implied with regard to professions, different patterns of mental focusing are also promoted by different cognitive subcultures within the same society. Indeed, that is also true of different "styles" of mental focusing. Consider, for example, the rigid, "no nonsense" style of focusing (most distinctively characterized by a sharp, clear-cut distinction between what is considered relevant and irrelevant) that is so pervasive in law (as evident from the high frequency of "Objection, your honor" interjections in courtroom discourse) and science (as evident from the explicit effort to manipulate variables in a highly controlled, decontextualized manner in scientific experiments). It certainly contrasts with the considerably more "fluid" style of mental focusing so distinctively characteristic of detectives, who look for clues *every*where, as well as landscape designers and social workers, who are specifically trained to consider context.

Given all this, it is hardly surprising that our mental horizons are often contested. Thus, while many of us basically consider animals morally irrelevant, animal-rights activists explicitly condemn such a fundamentally anthropocentric stance as morally narrow-minded. Similarly, whereas most of us envision a sharp mental fence separating art from life, there are some artists who purposefully try to blur the conventional distinction between the artistic and the real by producing "environmental" art that is virtually inseparable from its surroundings. In marked contrast to conventional paintings, urban grafitti, for example, are left deliberately unframed so as to fully blend in visually with their "background."[24]

Political disputes over whether or not race ought to be considered a factor in electoral redistricting or the extent to which the state is morally responsible for the welfare of undocumented aliens living within its borders serve as further examples, as do cultural battles over the place of women in the history of Western literature. Interpersonal skirmishes over whether or not one's lover's sexual whereabouts outside one's bed are one's "business"[25] or whether or not to raise a particular issue in a heated family argument are likewise instances of essentially cognitive battles over what should be considered relevant and what should remain disregarded "in the background."

That our mental horizons are for the most part neither natural nor logical is also evident from the fact that they quite often shift with time. It was only a few decades ago, after all, that smoking a cigarette was considered a "background" activity which others around one might very well fail to even notice! In a similar vein, whereas only two generations ago Americans were still taught to regard the color of one's skin as particularly relevant to one's social standing, nowadays they are taught to deliberately *dis*regard it.

Our moral horizons, too, keep shifting, thus incorporating into our current sphere of moral concern certain objects that were once excluded. Legal rights, for example, are now being extended to social categories whose legal standing was not so long ago utterly unthinkable (children, prisoners, the insane).[26] Only two centuries ago, women were likewise considered politically irrelevant, and when Mary Wollstonecraft published her *Vindication of the Rights of Women*, a distinguished Cambridge professor rebutted with a satirical *Vindication of the Rights of Brutes!*[27] Along similar lines, only recently have Americans become morally concerned about the thousands of Asians and Africans who die every year from famine and disease. And while many of us today are genuinely worried about what we are doing to our forests and rivers, we should keep in mind that, at least in the West, such "environmental" moral awareness is a relatively recent phenomenon.

Historical shifts in our mental horizons are sometimes also the result of major breakthroughs in science. After all, it is specifically as someone living in the twentieth century that I notice "Freudian" slips, which, prior to the publication of *The Psychopathology of Everyday Life* less than a century ago,[28] had always been largely unnoticed. My particular historical location also accounts for my explicit awareness of infant sexuality. Although infants clearly did not start masturbating only since Freud, it was nevertheless his writings that first prompted us to notice the fact that they do, to which we were practically blind before him.

Consider also the discovery of the asteroids in the early nineteenth century.[29] From a strictly technical standpoint, they definitely could have been noticed earlier. Yet it was William Herschel's dramatic discovery of Uranus in 1781, the first discovery of a "new" planet in several millennia, that mentally prepared an entire generation of astronomers to start finding additional ones.[30] Only their new cognitive sensitivity, indeed, can account for the rather rapid discovery of the four largest asteroids by three different astronomers within only twenty-six years of the discovery of Uranus.

Consider also the tremendous "optical" impact of Edward Hall's pioneering work in proxemics[31] on the social sciences, as evident from the voluminous research on the social organization of distance in face-to-face interaction that almost immediately followed the publication of *The Hidden Dimension* in the mid-1960s. Such a dramatic shift from irrelevance to relevance was particularly remarkable considering the fact that, prior to Hall, practically no one had ever been systematically attentive to this highly ubiquitous as well as visible dimension of human interaction (which accounts, of course, for the book's provocative title).

Hence the tremendous significance of cognitive revolutions that literally alter the shape of our phenomenal world by sensitizing us to things we have hitherto ignored. Indeed, such revolutions often involve an entire "gestalt switch," whereby the relation between what we notice and what we ignore is practically reversed.[32] As someone once described the special contribution of Erving Goffman to the study of social interaction, "like the hidden face in the picture, it's not hard to see, once it's pointed out. Goffman not only sees it, but makes the rest of us see it too."[33]

Yet while our mental focusing patterns are for the most part neither natural nor logical, they are not strictly personal either. In other words, they usually characterize not particular individuals but members of particular "optical" communities. Thus, it is specifically as a sociologist that one becomes desensitized to the aesthetic aspect of fashion and as a liberal late-twentieth-century American that one purposefully disregards the color of people's skin. Along similar lines, it is not just that particular individuals with contrasting focusing "styles" end up in law and landscape design but also that lawyers and landscape designers are differently *socialized* in how to focus their attention.

Separating the relevant from the irrelevant is for the most part a social act performed by members of particular "optical" communities who have been specifically socialized to disattend certain things as part of the process of adopting the distinctive "outlook" of their community.[34] In other words, we *learn* what to ignore, and only then does its irrelevance strike us as natural or "logical." Being socialized involves learning that players' age, sex, and weight, for example, are totally irrelevant in dominoes, Monopoly, and Parcheesi yet highly relevant in soccer, tennis, and boxing, respectively.[35] It likewise involves learning what one can disregard when one goes to an auction or a track meet.

Our moral horizons, too, are acquired socially through a process of learning. The fact that many young children are totally oblivious to the conventional moral distinction between humans and all other living creatures, for example, makes it quite clear that such a distinction is neither natural nor logical. To my son, saving tigers, gorillas, and other endangered species is still as morally pressing as saving human lives. Like so many other young readers of *Charlotte's Web* and *Bambi,* he clearly has not learned yet how to curb his moral attention in a socially appropriate manner.

Along similar lines, it is certainly not our personal feelings alone that make us concerned about some war casualties more than others (children more than adults, women more than men, humans more than birds). After all, only through being socialized does one come to know whether the concern about feeding one's dog should come before or only after the concern about feeding the homeless, or whether one ought to be more concerned about the well-being of fellow American businessmen in Southeast Asia or Southeast Asian refugees living in one's own neighborhood. By the same token, to many people who grew up in Nazi Germany, objecting to experiments with the retarded or with Jews would have probably seemed as odd as objecting to experiments with monkeys or rats seems to many of us today.

———

It is well known that we usually pay more attention to things that "fit" the mental schemas we use to make sense of the world (such as common stereotypes) than to those that are inconsistent with them.[36] Somewhat less noted, however, is the fact that many of those schemas are grounded in "optical" traditions we learn as part of our cognitive socialization.

The considerable extent to which thought communities' specific cognitive "biases" affect what their members come to notice[37] is quite evident in science. After all, only after having been "optically" socialized in a particular way do physicists, for example, come to notice certain objects, structures, and patterns which only other physicists can "see." By the same token, it is only radiologists' special professional training that enables them to notice on X rays and sonograms certain pathological formations which no one else can. The facts observed by scientists are not available to just anyone who happens to look at the world. Rather, they are a product of the particular way in which observers' attention is directed as a result of specific cognitive "intentions"[38] they acquire during their professional "optical" socialization.

Consider even the basic decision of what to observe. When astronomers, biologists, or radiologists approach a telescope, a microscope, or an X ray, for example, they do not simply look. The fact that they choose one of numerous possible probes shows that even at that stage they already have at least a vague notion of what ought to constitute the main focus of their observations and what they can disregard as irrelevant. (In fact, even the choice of the specific optical instrument they use forces them to notice certain things while ignoring others. After all, one would not try to probe the surface of the moon with a microscope, or the structure of a blood cell with a telescope.)[39] By the same token, when a sociologist decides to examine the relation between students' marital status and the amount of time it takes them to complete their studies and get their degree, her decision also presupposes an implicit decision on her part to regard their weight and the color of their hair, for example, as irrelevant. In fact, she will most probably not even try to control for those variables, in marked contrast to her deliberate efforts to control for their age and grade point average, for example. Before I began studying sociology, I certainly did not see social life the way I "see" it today. Only by having gone through a long process of professional "optical" socialization did I come to develop unmistakably sociological cognitive sensitivities to the conventional, the impersonal, the collective, and the normative. Along similar lines, only by undergoing such socialization and acquiring a distinctive "sociological imagination" do sociologists come to "see" labor markets, power structures, support networks, and stratification systems.

Such "optical" socialization takes place at the level of entire professions as well as particular "schools" or "paradigms"[40] within professions. As a result, one finds considerable differences in mental focusing between doctors and social workers as well as between different "kinds" of doctors. For example, whereas a conventional ear, nose, and throat doctor is unlikely to ask a patient who complains about pain in his ear even a single question about his knee, essentially treating it a priori as irrelevant, a more "holistic" practitioner may very well do that, having been specifically socialized to regard *every* part of the human body as systemically related to *all* the others.

When I was a graduate student, I was once invited to attend a seminar on group dynamics taught by Robert Freed Bales and, along with his students, observed a group of people interacting in his social psychology laboratory. Later, when we compared the notes we had taken while observing the ongoing interaction, I was struck by how very little overlap there was between them—whereas mine were almost all about performance strategies and the organization of social space, theirs were mostly about subtle power dynamics within the group. Indeed, such focal discrepancy was quite understandable given the fact that, at the time, I was studying with (and heavily influenced by) Erving Goffman, whose own conception of social interaction was considerably different from that of Bales. Using two rather different mental lenses grounded in two quite distinct "optical" traditions of approaching social interaction, we were actually observing two altogether different social situations!

Not only does our social environment provide us with a general idea of what we can disattend, it very often also tells us what we *should* repress from our consciousness and ignore. In other words, there is an important (though relatively unexplored) normative dimension to relevance and irrelevance. Indeed, probably the main reason that our own focusing patterns seem so natural or "logical" to us is that they are usually normatively binding.

Ignoring something normally involves more than just failure on one's part to notice it. Ignoring another person's stutter, limp, or harelip, for example, is usually an active display of tact rather than the result of simply failing to notice it.[41] Indeed, we very often *do* notice certain things which we nevertheless learn to tune out as irrelevant. Rather than simply not notice them, we deliberately *dis*attend them.

What we consider relevant is usually defined as such in accordance with particular *norms of focusing* that we learn as part of our "optical" socialization and which lead us to regard certain parts of reality as mere "background." Thus, for example, it is unmistakably social norms of tact rather than any natural constraints on our hearing that often lead us to try to disregard highly personal conversations taking place around us in crowded subways and cafeterias. By the same token, when we watch a soccer game, it is social norms of focusing that determine who is considered a full-fledged participant and who is regarded as a mere bystander whom we can basically ignore. It is likewise social "*rules* of irrelevance"[42] that make bureaucrats who screen job applications exclude applicants' sex or race from their official considerations and that determine that whereas athletes' age and size are considered relevant in sports, their sexual orientation and political affiliation are not.[43]

Noticing the attention-"worthy" and ignoring the irrelevant are not just spontaneous personal acts, since they are always performed by people who are also members of particular thought communities with particular normative traditions of focusing. Like the unmistakably social "feeling rules" that make flight attendants seem so much more pleasant than bill collectors,[44] norms of focusing (which similarly make holistic healers seem so much more broad-minded than conventional ear, nose, and throat doctors) clearly affect us not as individuals but as social beings.

As one would expect, the normative delineation of our attention and concern is one of the most insidious forms of social control.[45] Through the various norms of focusing we internalize as part of our "optical" socialization, society essentially controls which thoughts even "cross" our minds.

The ability to help determine what others consider relevant and what they basically disregard is an important aspect of social power. After all, it is parents who teach their children (and not children who teach their parents) what is considered irrelevant, and teachers who determine by the readings they assign as well as by what they include on the examinations they give what their students come to regard as attention-worthy. In a somewhat similar vein, it is judges who dictate to jurors what they should officially ignore and one's superiors who usually determine what is included on (and thus also what is excluded from) the agendas of the meetings one attends.

Yet just as critical are the more tacit (and therefore somewhat less obvious) manifestations of such sociomental control. Consider, for example, the role of mass media in shaping the scope of our political as well as cultural attention.[46] As evident from the considerable difference between the political and cultural horizons of *New York Times* and *New York Post* readers, for example, those horizons are often a by-product of the kind of information we get from our newspapers, radio, or television. In fact, those media also affect how long we attend any particular news story. After all, as soon as they stop covering it, we usually forget about it altogether.

Consider also the social control of intellectual attention in academia.[47] It is their professional community that usually rewards academics for restricting their intellectual concerns to the inevitably parochial confines of their particular "field" of scholarship (or an even more narrowly defined "area" of concentration within it) and practically penalizes undisciplined transgressors who defy its restrictive norms of focusing and try to venture beyond those confines into the intellectual turfs of other disciplines. Thus, it is the sociological community, for example, that tacitly pressures me to curb my personal interest in ancient history and parapsychology and to keep asking myself constantly whether what I am doing professionally indeed falls within the conventional boundaries of what is considered "sociology." Such pressure, however tacit, typically involves the use of intellectual blinders quite similar to those that close our aesthetic horizons and have kept my former "classical" piano teacher, for example, from even exposing himself to the music of "jazz" piano greats such as Bud Powell or Thelonious Monk.[48]

Finally, consider the unmistakably cognitive underpinnings of our erotic sentiments, as manifested in the way we tacitly refrain from even considering certain objects as potential sexual partners because we basically regard them as erotically irrelevant. If we do not usually perceive infants, dogs, orchids, or our best friends' spouses as sexually attractive, it is mainly because they "belong" in social categories that, given our society's norms of erotic focusing,[49] are excluded from the universe of objects that we consider erotically relevant. In fact, desiring members of some of these categories is often considered perverse.[50] As a result of such institutional desexualization, very few men, for example, consciously perceive other men as sexually attractive even when they are particularly aroused, thereby exemplifying the tremendous power of society to affect our taste, feelings, and moral senses by essentially controlling the gates to our minds.

4 /

The Social Division of
the World

Not only does society affect what actually enters our minds, it also influences the way it is then organized inside our heads. In other words, it also affects the way we classify the world.

Like focusing and perceiving, classifying is a universal mental act that we all perform as human beings. Like leopards, turtles, and storks, *every* person, for example, distinguishes that which is edible ("food") from that which is inedible. By the same token, like rabbits, antelopes, and blue jays, *all* humans distinguish that which is dangerous from that which is safe.

At the same time, classifying is also a personal act that we perform as individuals. The lines we draw between the books we consider interesting and boring or between the songs we consider happy and sad, for example, often vary in their "location" from one person to another. So, for that matter, does the extent to which we generally regard our professional life as integrated with our personal life.[1]

Yet classifying is also a social act that we perform not as individuals or as human beings but *as social beings*, and although some ways of dividing the world are obviously personal or universal, some are unmistakably social. After all, the way we happen to draw the line between "classical" and "popular" music or between "drama" and "comedy" is remarkably similar to the way others do, despite the fact that it is neither natural nor logical. So is the way we cut up the world into conventional islands of meaning[2] such as "Serbs" and "Croats," or "liberals" and "conservatives," or the way we separate "religion" from "ideology," the proper from the improper, the 1980s from the 1990s, or the "serious" from the merely "playful." In a similar vein, note that while it is quite common for people to talk to their cats, name them, kiss them, and feature them quite prominently in their family photo albums, rarely do they do any of those things with the mice they find in their kitchens or with their wallets. Such difference, of course, is a result of the way we usually classify nonhuman objects in terms of their perceived proximity to us. Yet such "proximity" is entirely conventional, since cats, after all, are not inherently closer to us than either mice or the wallets we carry on us almost constantly.[3] By the same token, when we see people eating sardines and ducks yet never goldfish or parrots, we are likewise seeing society and its cognitive norms in action.

Perhaps the most striking evidence of the social nature of classification is the fact that different cultures often carve out of the same reality somewhat different islands of meaning. Not everybody who is considered "black" in Utah or New Hampshire, for example, would necessarily be regarded as such in Puerto Rico or Brazil.[4] Nor, for that matter, are "cancer," "depression," or "viral infection" universal diagnostic categories.[5]

Consider also, in this regard, the indisputably social foundations of our basic notions of edibility. Although all cultures indeed distinguish edible from inedible objects, they often vary with respect to the specific contents of those general categories. The same raw fish which many Americans consider inedible, for example, is actually regarded as a delicacy in Japan. By the same token, it is unmistakably conventional *norms of classification* that lead Westerners to eat pigs and cows (which Muslims and Hindus strictly abhor) yet avoid bats, horses, and dogs.

The distinction between the sexually accessible and inaccessible is likewise universal (virtually all cultures, for example, have some form of an incest taboo), yet the specific delineation of those who are considered sexually off-limits often varies from one culture to another. (Cousins, for example, are considered off-limits in some cultures yet quite accessible in others.) In a similar vein, whereas the distinctions between the intimate and the socially distant as well as between personal and public space are universal, cultures nevertheless vary with respect to "where" they actually draw the lines between those general categories.[6]

Furthermore, there are certain mental distinctions that are made by some cultures but not others. Not every culture, for example, distinguishes "real" work from volunteer work, "salary" from "bonus,"[7] eating from "snacking," and "fiction" from nonfiction. Nor does every culture mentally isolate "war crimes," "table manners," or "sexual harassment" as distinct behavioral as well as moral categories. Indeed, the semantic range of what constitutes a single word in one language often corresponds to the combined range of several separate words in another.[8] (Thus, whereas the single French word *conscience* means both "conscience" and "consciousness," there are actually separate words in Navajo for blankets that are folded and ones that are spread out, for water in lakes and in buckets, and for dogs who are sitting and standing.)[9] Such lexical inconsistencies have considerable cognitive implications, since it is much easier to isolate an island of meaning from its mental surroundings when there is a special word available to denote it.[10] It took me (a native Hebrew speaker) many years to learn to "see" the unmistakably conventional mental gaps,[11] so obvious to native English-speakers, separating "jam" from "jelly," "blinds" from "shutters," and "garbage" from "trash."

Such variance has traditionally led us to look down on other cultures' classification systems as backward or "confused,"[12] yet it can also help us recognize the conventional nature of our own instead of taking it for granted as we normally do.[13] After all, the very people we consider savages might actually find it rather peculiar that we somehow "fail" to mentally differentiate fathers' brothers from mothers' sisters' husbands (thereby regarding both as "uncles"), or that we lump first and third "cousins" or maternal and paternal "grandfathers" together in a single category. They might also find the logic of becoming sentimentally attached to hamsters and gerbils while at the same time poisoning rats and mice somewhat bizarre. Such blatant cross-cultural inconsistencies certainly help us realize that our own particular way of cutting up the world into supposedly distinct mental chunks is by no means the only "logical" way to do it.

Not only do different cultures carve different archipelagos of meaning out of the same reality; they very often also promote altogether different "styles" of cutting up the world.[14]

Some cultures, for example, promote rigid-mindedness, a highly inflexible mind-set distinctively characterized by strict adherence to a purist, "either/or" logic. Such cultures typically cherish razor-sharp, clear-cut distinctions and are generally averse to ambiguous hybrids and in-betweens that might challenge the perceived mutual exclusivity of their categories. As one would expect, they are highly preoccupied with boundaries and extremely obsessed with preserving mental purity and avoiding mental contamination.[15]

A classic example of such a rigid-minded culture is Orthodox Judaism. Orthodox Jews' particular obsession with boundaries and distinctions is evidenced in their strong aversion to mixing categories. (Indeed, two tractates of the Mishnah, the compiled rabbinical interpretations of scriptural ordinances, are actually named "hybrids" [Kilaim] and "mixings" [Erubin] and are devoted exclusively to boundary-related matters.) Their firm commitment to endogamy (to the point of actually mourning, and even mock-burying, group members who marry non-Jews), strong aversion to zoological anomalies, careful dietary separation of meat and milk products, and strict prohibition of garments made of both linen and wool are clear manifestations of the rigid Orthodox Jewish style of cutting up the world into discrete islands of meaning that are never to "touch" one another. So, of course, are the strict abomination of transvestism (which explicitly blurs the distinction between masculinity and femininity) and the rather conspicuous absence of ambiguous mythical hybrids (such as the mermaid or the centaur) that might blur the distinction between human and animal. No wonder this culture has thought up a purist God who actually spends the first three of only six days he has in which to create a world just making distinctions![16]

Somewhat similar in its uncompromisingly rigid style of dividing the world is the Gypsy culture, which is just as obsessed with purity and averse to mental promiscuity and ambiguity. Like Orthodox Jews, Gypsies practice strict endogamy, and their fear of mental contamination leads them to avoid any food prepared—as well as any furniture used—by non-Gypsies. Their extreme concern about pollution is likewise manifested in their strict avoidance of any contact between the upper and lower parts of their bodies, to the point of actually using separate soaps, washbasins, and towels for washing them. Gypsies also have a strong aversion to animals that blur the distinction between their interior and exterior by either licking their fur (cats, dogs) or shedding their skin (lizards, snakes), and are particularly fond of the hedgehog, a creature that, given its bristly physique, is one of the most glaring icons of insularity.[17]

At the same time, however, there are other cultures that promote somewhat contrasting styles of organizing the world in one's mind. Some cultures specifically promote fuzzy-mindedness, a virtually structureless mind-set distinctively characterized by an aversion to any boundary that might prevent mental interpenetration.[18] Others promote flexible-mindedness, a pronouncedly fluid mind-set distinctively characterized by a "both/and" (rather than an "either/or") logic of classification that strongly rejects pigeonholing.[19] As one would expect, such cultures are quite comfortable with, and indeed encourage, ambiguity. Thus, among the Navaho, one typically finds a somewhat fuzzy clan structure, a highly reverential attitude towards hermaphrodites, and a strong aversion to any form of closure in artistic design.[20] Similarly, among the Eskimo, one finds rather fluid definitions of both family and gender, as manifested in extremely flexible residential and adoption arrangements as well as in the option parents are sometimes given to raise their daughters as boys.[21]

Yet it is not only different cultures that promote different styles of organizing the world in one's mind. Even within the same culture there are different social domains distinctively associated with rigid-, fuzzy-, or flexible-mindedness.[22]

Consider religion, which is actually where our notions of purity, pollution, and contamination originally developed long before they acquired their present hygienic associations.[23] One of the distinctive cognitive characteristics of religion is the rigid manner in which it usually divides the world into two ("sacred" and "profane") compartments that are perceived as mutually exclusive.[24] It is specifically in order to ensure that those two compartments would indeed never "touch" each other (and thereby protect the sacred from being "contaminated" by the profane) that sanctuaries and holidays, for example, are created, along with numerous taboos on touching, looking at, or even mentioning the sacred.[25]

The distinctive cognitive characteristics of bureaucracy are remarkably similar. Whereas religion tries to keep the sacred separate from the profane, bureaucracy promotes a similar mental segregation of the "official" from the unofficial. It is bureaucracy, for example, that is responsible for the strict exclusion of "personal" matters from public discourse (and, thus, for the ritual separation of official from personal stationery and of the formally printed from the informally handwritten) as well as for the very careful separation of public monies from officials' private assets. It likewise promotes a rigid distinction between public and private space and time, thereby separating office from home and confining professional commitments to strictly delineated "duty periods."[26] Not surprisingly, such a sharp break between officials' "on-duty" and "off-duty" time often coincides with an equally rigid distinction between co-workers and friends.[27] Like the separation of "business" from personal correspondence and public from private equipment, both are products of the same rigid mind.[28]

At the same time, however, there are other social domains that promote precisely the opposite style of organizing the world in one's mind. Art, intimacy, and play are some classic examples of such fuzzy-minded domains.

Art often promotes mental promiscuity by essentially defying the conventional partitioning of reality into discrete, mutually exclusive mental compartments.[29] The explicit attempt to blur the very distinction between figure and ground by renouncing sharply delineated contours (either graphically, as in the hazy landscapes produced by Turner and Seurat, or sonically, as in harmony), for example, is a perfect manifestation of such an essentially fuzzy-minded approach to the world.[30] By the same token, only in the world of art are explicit images of gender transgression accepted and even revered (consider the tremendous success of Marlene Dietrich, David Bowie, Michael Jackson, Jean Poiret's *La Cage aux Folles,* and Neil Jordan's *The Crying Game*) by people who would never accept the mental fusion of masculinity and femininity elsewhere.

Such fuzzy-mindedness is even more pronounced in intimacy, where boundaries between separate, insular selves typically melt away.[31] After all, it is the perceived gaps between mental entities that make them seem discrete, and eliminating the actual physical gap between lovers during sexual intercourse literally blurs their respective body contours, thereby also obliterating the discrete, insular selves they symbolically envelop. Essentially blending two separate selves in a single union, love, too, is antithetical to insularity, and sharing one's personal space, possessions, or information about oneself (arguably the three most guarded tokens of individuality) is indeed one of the most effective ways of displaying it. Not surprisingly, it is also in intimacy that all other social divisions are typically ignored and the widest social chasms most easily overcome.

Nothing defies our division into separate nations, social classes, ethnic groups, or religious communities more forcefully than intermarriage (which is indeed, along with sex in general, typically abhorred by the rigid mind).[32]

Play, too, promotes fuzzy-mindedness.[33] Consider the way jokes and riddles often challenge the very notion of discrete islands of meaning by deliberately juxtaposing, or even fusing, mental contexts which we normally regard as separate.[34] Consider also the pronounced display of mental promiscuity in ludic environments such as the circus (where dogs eating at tables, apes riding bicycles, and horses playing soccer basically mock the conventional mental gulf separating humans from animals)[35] or carnival (where practically all social status barriers are temporarily obliterated).[36] An irreverent assault on our conventional classifications is also one of the most distinctive characteristics of humor.[37]

Play also promotes *flexible*-mindedness by highlighting the fluid, plastic nature of identity. One such instance is the featured display of multiple meanings (and therefore ambiguity) in puns, card games (where a six of spades can be used as a six in one series and as a spade in another), and "knock-knock" jokes.[38] Another is the way things are turned into other things in magic shows, or the way actors (Peter Sellers, Louis de Funès, Robin Williams) rapidly assume and discard different personal identities when they do comic impressions. Stretching the conventional boundaries of the self by essentially transforming oneself into somebody else is also a major feature of ludic environments such as the costume party, where personal as well as social identities are quite casually assumed and discarded (thereby also mocking ethnic, gender, occupational, age, and other conventional social distinctions) through cross-dressing and masquerading.[39]

The social nature of classification is also evident from the fact that the lines we draw and the distinctions we make often change over time. Ninety years ago, for example, opiates were still considered legal drugs in America, and the idea that smokers, anti-abortionists, or homosexuals might someday constitute distinct political categories would have probably struck most Americans as preposterous as the idea of granting such status to volleyball fans, philosophy majors, or people who take their coffee with cream might to us today. By the same token, it is useful to remember that the seemingly timeless distinction between "high" and popular culture is relatively recent,[40] that the fine line separating "whites" from "blacks" in America has already shifted many times over the past two hundred years,[41] and that the precise location of the point marking the beginning of life is still shifting today.[42] Just as fickle are the fine lines separating the playful from the serious and art from life. Unlike the ancient Romans, for example,[43] modern-day Italians do not expect wrestlers to actually die in contests and would never execute real-life convicts as part of a theatrical performance.

General "styles" of organizing the world in one's mind also change over time, with different historical periods often promoting altogether different mind-sets.[44] The general modern (as well as "postmodern") bent towards fuzzy-mindedness is a perfect case in point.

A fuzzy-minded vision of the world is quite evident in the general modern aversion to conventional social divisions. Such an aversion is manifested in the movement towards racial desegregation, in the explicit feminist effort to "degenderize" human relations, as well as in the relentless Marxist attempt to create a classless society. It can likewise be seen in the efforts of the community mental health system to integrate the mentally ill into the rest of society[45] and in the "integrative" philosophy of management, which downplays traditional hierarchical and departmental divisions within organizations.[46]

Modernity also promotes the obliteration of traditional group divisions at the macrosocial level. When Americans of Scandinavian descent eat pizza, Nigerians play soccer, and Koreans listen to rock music, the very notion of insular "cultures" becomes obsolete. The world keeps moving towards greater integration of historically insulated political, economic, and communication systems. The current proliferation of a global market economy with multinational corporations, along with the development of global communication networks such as the Internet, is clearly making such traditional categories less and less meaningful every day.[47]

Such an essentially fuzzy-minded view of the world can also be seen in modern design, as evident from the modern fascination with glass, which basically blurs the fundamental distinction between inside and outside by allowing them to visually interpenetrate each other.[48] A somewhat similar craving for visual fluidity also underlies the modern idea of "open" design, as manifested in the split-level house as well as in the transformation of traditional rooms into semi-open "areas."[49]

Such "fuzzy thinking" is also central to modern art, as evident from the explicit cubist assault on conventional outlines[50] and the introduction of the "stream of consciousness" style (which defies the conventional partitioning of reality into discrete mental compartments) into modern literature. Furthermore, modern art often tries to blur the conventional distinction between art and life by allowing the artistic and the "real" to literally interpenetrate each other. Such an effort is evident from the explicit modernist attempt to blur the conventional distinction between artistic and "real" time, as exemplified by poems (such as some of Cummings's) that begin in the middle of a word, theatrical performances (such as Pirandello's *Tonight We Improvise*) that continue through the intermission, and "happenings."[51] It can also be seen in the somewhat parallel attempt to blur the conventional distinction between artistic and "real" space, as exemplified by Mondrian's truncated squares and rectangles, which visually pull the viewer outside the painting, or the environmental theater, which basically obliterates the traditional distinction between house and stage.[52] And it is also evident from the modernist attempt to blur the conventional distinction between artistic and "real" objects, as manifested in the collage as well as in artistic installations that feature natural processes.[53]

The works of Cummings, Joyce, Picasso, Pirandello, and Mondrian are distinctively modern. So, of course, are glass architecture, multinational corporations, and the Internet. Nor is it pure coincidence that the "open school" (with its movable walls, highly unstructured curriculum, and flexible age-grouping),[54] the "happening," and the idea of "open marriage"[55] all evolved around the same point in human history. They are, I suspect, far more closely related than may appear at first glance.

Indeed, we might think of them as different manifestations of a single, unmistakably fuzzy-minded vision of the world. The same fundamental aversion to distinctions underlies the movement towards racial desegregation, the "holistic" critique of conventional Western medicine, the feminist attempt to "degenderize" society, and the collage. What distinctively characterizes the modern (as well as "postmodern") way of thinking "is not just another redrawing of the cultural map—the moving of a few disputed borders . . . but an alteration of the principles of mapping. Something is happening to the way we think about the way we think . . ."[56]

Yet the lines we draw and the distinctions we make also vary across cognitive subcultures within the same culture during the same period. Even within contemporary American society, meat-eaters clearly draw the line between the edible and the inedible somewhat differently than do vegetarians. Indeed, even within the same culture, mental partitions that seem almost inevitable to one cognitive subculture may not even be noticed by others. The distinction made by some college students between "stylish radical-chic" and "granola" lesbians, for example, is usually lost on older alumni, "to whom the shadings of lesbian politics are as irrelevant as the difference between Sodom and Gomorrah."[57] And while some professions may envision an actual gulf separating their members' personal and professional lives, others seem to regard the distinction between the two as somewhat fuzzy.[58]

As one might expect, such diversity may generate considerable discord. And indeed, as we carve distinct islands of meaning out of the world around us, the actual "location" as well as the very existence of the mental divides separating them from one another is often disputed.

"Border disputes"[59] over the particular location of mental partitions range from academic debates over the boundaries between species[60] to legislative battles over driving speed limits and acceptable levels of pollution.[61] They include, for example, political as well as moral disputes over the specifics of a country's immigration policy or over the fine line separating pretty from "provocative" dresses or R-rated from X-rated films. They likewise include cultural battles over the definitions of science[62] and work (such as the ones over the status of UFOs and housework) as well as curricular skirmishes over what ought to be included in a society's literary "canon."

Consider also, in this regard, border disputes over the temporal delineation of life. Conflicting medical and legal definitions of the fine line separating life from death[63] often lead to fierce moral battles over the point at which doctors may turn off life-sustaining equipment. Defining the actual moment when life begins is likewise at the heart of the heated political debate over whether or not abortion ought to be considered homicide.[64]

Yet the politics of classification[65] involve major cognitive battles not only over the particular "location" of mental divides but also over their very existence (that is, not only over what specifically ought to be included in a society's literary "canon" but also over whether or not such a "canon" should exist in the first place). Nation-states, for example, usually ignore political borders drawn by separatists, and the fine line between erotic art and pornography is similarly challenged by conservatives as well as radical feminists. Governments and dissidents also engage in passionate "classification struggles"[66] over the fine line between "satire" and explicit political protest, and animal rights crusaders and scientists debate the legitimacy of invoking a "research" frame to justify the killing of animals in laboratories.

It is hardly surprising that the distinctions we make actually vary across cultures (as well as subcultures), change over time, and are often disputed. After all, the lines we envision separating one "thing" from another are not as natural as they may seem, despite our tendency to break up the world into sharply delineated islands of meaning. In reality things are rarely ever "cut off with an axe."[67] Indeed, nature usually "refuses to conform to our craving for clear lines of demarcation; she loves twilight zones."[68]

Although we may carve in our minds seemingly distinct neighborhoods, countries, and continents out of space, in the real world there *are* no natural divides separating New York's Chinatown from Little Italy, Morocco from Algeria, or even Europe from Asia.[69] Nor are forests, mountains, or deserts sharply delineated in nature. Even the so-called coastlines that separate land from sea are not real lines.[70]

Consider also the supposedly discrete mental chunks (days, months, seasons, centuries) we carve in our minds out of time.[71] In reality, days and nights are always connected by inevitably ambiguous twilights and dawns. By the same token, no natural divides separate August from September, "winter" from "spring," or the twentieth century from the twenty-first.

This is also true of the supposedly discrete clusters into which we normally lump people in our minds. In the real world, there *are* no lines dividing Persians from Armenians, Christians from Muslims, or "blacks" from "whites." Nor is there any natural divide separating normals from "perverts," "blue-collar" from "white-collar" workers,[72] or the "sane" from the insane.[73]

Despite our obvious tendency to compartmentalize, reality is essentially fluid. Instead of sharply delineated, insular chunks unambiguously separated by natural divides, it is made up of vague, blurred-edged essences that "spill over" into one another.[74] Distinctions between "things" are not as sharp as (and the actual transitions among them far more gradual than) we may envision. As one might expect, the categories in which we organize the world in our minds are therefore also not as sharply delineated (that is, "well-defined") as we may perhaps envision them. Membership in those categories is only a matter of degree, and the transition from member to nonmember, therefore, rather gradual.[75] The mental outlines of the categories "light" and "dark," for example, certainly overlap, as do those of the categories "desk" and "table," or "soft" and "loud." The transition from "masculine" to "feminine" is likewise gradual (and the differences within each gender, therefore, as significant as those between them),[76] since even the distribution of purely physiological male and female features is rarely ever absolutely bipolar. (Although the female body is, on the average, somewhat less muscular and hairy than the male's, many women happen to have a more muscular and hairy body than many men.) Nor, for that matter, are the conventional distinctions between "blue" and "purple," "cup" and "mug," or "alto" and "soprano" any sharper.

Breaking up the world into discrete, quasi-insular mental chunks is accomplished largely through language.[77] As we assign them distinct labels, we actually come to perceive "four-star" hotels as qualitatively different from "three-star" hotels, and "herbs" such as dill and parsley as significantly distinct from mere "leaves," which we would never allow on our plates. (At the same time, it is our ability to assign things a common label that also helps us connect them in our minds. Only the availability of the category "pre-Columbian," for example, enables us to lump together[78] the Olmec and Aztec civilizations, which actually flourished some 2,000 years apart from one another.) It is language that helps us differentiate in our minds "this week" from "last week," seventeen-year-old "minors" from eighteen-year-old "adults," and "the 1950s" from "the 1960s."[79] It is likewise language that enables us to carve out of physical continua supposedly discrete mental chunks such as "hot" and "cold" or "fetus" and "baby"[80] as well as to think about "premenstruation" as a distinct phase of the human female reproductive cycle.[81]

Language, of course, is highly impersonal,[82] yet although its categories are by no means products of our own personal imagination, they are not natural either. Since it is one of the foundations of our social reality, we tend to forget that language itself rests on social convention and to regard the mental divisions it introduces as real. When we label our world, we often commit the fallacy of misplaced concreteness and regard the purely conventional mental gaps separating North America from Central America or business from pleasure as if they were part of nature.[83]

It is important, therefore, to avoid the tendency to reify the conventional islands of meaning in which we organize the world in our minds and to remember that the gaps we envision separating them from one another are purely mental. In the real world, after all, there *are* no actual divides separating the moral from the immoral or the public from the private. Mental divisions as well as the entities they help delineate have no ontological status whatsoever. It is we ourselves who organize reality in separate mental compartments.[84]

Classification, thus, is a process of actively "sculpting"[85] islands of meaning rather than simply identifying already-existing natural ones. Yet while they may not exist in the real world "out there," they are not purely subjective. Although it is a mind that breaks up the world into separate chunks, it is not always an individual's mind. We may not all cut up the world identically, but the chunks we carve out of it are nonetheless remarkably similar to those carved out by others around us. Thus, when we draw lines and make distinctions, we do so not only as human beings or as individuals, but also as social beings.

5 /

Social Meanings

Like perception, the process of classification clearly underscores the role of meaning in human cognition. Nowhere, however, is that role as explicitly evident as when we examine the way we use *symbols*.

Using symbols presupposes a mental association of two elements, one of which (the "signifier") is regarded as representing, or "standing for," the other (the "signified").[1] The meaning of a present, thus, is the personal affection it is supposed to represent. Convertible cars likewise may signify free-spiritedness, whereas cigars are often associated in our minds with virility.

When we regard something as a symbol, we are primarily concerned with what it represents, to the point where what it actually "means" sometimes overrides any functional significance it may otherwise have for us. Champagne, for example, is thus associated in our minds far more with celebrating than with simply quenching thirst. Long, polished fingernails likewise function primarily not as claws but as symbolic evidence of having reached a certain social status that protects one from the need to perform hard physical labor.[2]

Along similar lines, clothes become for us more than simply practical responses to weather conditions. Differences in clothing, for example, often signify differences between contrasting types of social space (home versus work),[3] time (sacred versus profane),[4] and ambiance (formal versus casual). Loosening one's tie or removing one's shoes may thus signify a switch from formality to informality, whereas opening a button in one's blouse may be "read" as an implicit invitation to one's bed. We likewise use clothes to signify various professional (military uniform), ethnic (sari), gender (nylon stockings), and political (pro-life T-shirt) identities.[5]

Like clothes, time, too, is loaded with extra-functional meanings. It is the distinctly symbolic significance of "lead time" (rather than just the practical fact that one may have other plans), for example, that may make one decline a "last-minute" invitation to a wedding or a prom, and the political symbolism of waiting that sometimes leads people to be purposefully late and let others "cool their heels" in order to humiliate them. When we specifically refrain from contacting someone "too soon," it is usually because of the way we associate frequency of contact with intimacy (which is also why switching from getting together every day to every other week is likely to be interpreted as indicative of some significant cooling off in a relationship).[6]

The mental association of a particular signifier with a particular signified may very well be the work of a particular individual. The meaning of our dreams, for example, is for the most part personal, and no respectable psychoanalyst would ever attempt to "decode" a dream without some significant input from the particular patient who dreamt it. Most symbolic associations, however, involve *shared* meanings and, as such, are not just personal. At the same time, they are not natural either. In fact, most meanings rest on conventional, *socio*mental associations of particular signifiers with particular signifieds.

To fully appreciate the unmistakably social nature of symbols, we need to compare them with other kinds of signs. It would be particularly useful, in this regard, to examine the extent to which the mental association of a particular signifier with the particular signified it represents is natural. That, of course, would allow us to establish "where" the meaning of any given sign falls between inevitability and conventionality.

As Figure 5.1 shows, approaching signification from this angle basically yields three major types of signs—the ones embodying the two polar extremes of absolute inevitability *(indicators)* and pure conventionality *(symbols)*, and an in-between composite of major elements of both *(icons)*.[7] The most striking contrast is the one between symbols and indicators, which are distinctively characterized by the intrinsic (and thus inevitable) nature of their association with what they represent. The semiotic relation between an indicator and what it signifies to us is absolutely natural and does not require any artificial mediation in the form of social convention.

Consider medical symptoms, those pieces of physical evidence we regard as "symptomatic," or "indicative," of particular diseases. The mental association of rectal bleeding with cancer of the colon or of certain blisters and the viral condition we call chicken pox, for example, has absolutely nothing to do with social convention. Nor does the association of smoke with fire, of daffodils with spring, of a fast heartbeat with excitement, or of the height of a mercury column in a glass tube with the temperature. Such connections are certainly not something for which we ourselves are in any way responsible.

Most of the signs we use in our daily life, however, are not indicators. Their association with what they are supposed to represent to

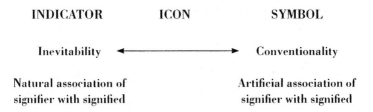

Figure 5.1. Types of signification

us involves a certain element of human intervention and, as such, is far from inevitable. The meaning of these signs is clearly extrinsic to them, an unmistakably artificial property added by social convention alone.

The artificial, conventional nature of all signs other than indicators is evident even in iconic representation, which still presupposes some physical resemblance between signifier and signified. After all, despite the obvious physical affinity between the cross and the actual shape of the crucified body of Christ, its mental association with Christianity is by no means inevitable and rests at least partly on social convention.[8] And whereas the smell of a rabbit inevitably denotes to predators an actual rabbit, the mental association of a conventional outline drawing of a rabbit with an actual rabbit already presupposes an element of socialization. (In fact, slightly shorter ears and a somewhat longer tail would immediately "transform" such a conventional rabbit into a conventional cat, despite the fact that no actual cat ever looks like a long-tailed, short-eared rabbit.)[9] Only humans, of course, seem to undergo such *semiotic socialization*, which explains why, despite the obviously great arousal power of nude photographs for humans, we would never expect a fox, for example, to actually be turned on by a mere picture (or any other iconic representation) of a vixen's body.

The contrast between indicators and signs whose meaning is less inevitable and more conventional becomes even more pronounced as we proceed from merely iconic to strictly symbolic modes of representation (whereby sexual arousal, for example, is generated not even by an actual picture of a naked body but through the mere use of "erotic" language to describe it). Unlike icons, symbols do not presuppose any physical affinity whatsoever between a signifier and what it is supposed to represent to us. It is the difference between an outline drawing of a rabbit and the word "rabbit," between the Roman numeral "III" and the mathematical sign "3," between a cross and the sound of a pipe organ.

In fact, the meaning of symbols is completely dissociated from their physical properties. Had we not been semiotically socialized to "read" clocks, for example, we would never be able to tell the time from the angle formed by a clock's hands. Nor would we be able to figure out that a rectangle with white, green, and red horizontal stripes "means" Bulgaria, or that the dove, which is in fact a rather unfriendly bird, has anything to do with peace.

Of all the signs we use, the mental association between signifier and signified is the least inevitable in symbols. Indeed, it is their absolutely artificial, conventional nature that distinguishes symbols from all other signs.[10]

Thus, if we are to understand the full meaning of a particular symbol, we cannot afford to consider its physical properties alone. A symbolic analysis of snakes that focuses strictly on their iconic "phallic" essence, for example, is inherently limited. Nor can we fully understand why widows wear black dresses if we focus only on the seemingly inevitable macabre nature of the color black.

In fact, the actual color of the dresses widows wear is not as symbolically significant as the fact that it so sharply contrasts with the color of the dresses *brides* wear. Indeed, the meaning of the colors of the dresses both brides and widows wear is the message they convey *together* about the fundamental cultural contrast between the social states of entering and exiting marriage for women.[11]

The meaning of symbols generally derives not from their own inherent properties but from the way they are semiotically positioned in our minds vis-à-vis other symbols. Thus, in order to understand how a particular symbol comes to be mentally associated with what it represents to us, we must first understand how it is related to other symbols we use. The critical relation, in this regard, is contrast or opposition, since a symbol basically derives its meaning from its *distinctive* features, those properties that distinguish it from other symbols.[12] In order to know what it is, we must therefore first find out what it is *not*. I once saw a man looking at two public restroom doors labeled "Bucks" and "Does" who muttered to himself, "I am not a doe, so I guess I am a buck." In order to understand the meaning of the word "man," for example, we first need to know whether it is used in contrast to "woman" (as in "this is definitely a man's job"), "child" (as in "for God's sake, act like a man"), "animal" (as in "when man started using language"), or "nature" (as in "man-made fibers").

Semantics, in short, is inseparable from syntactics. In order to fully understand the meaning of a symbol, we must transcend the narrow confines of a strictly semantic analysis and consider also the syntactic context within which it is structurally embedded (that is, the way it is semiotically contrasted in our minds with other symbols).[13]

A "semiotic square" may help us see more clearly the relational nature of symbols, the fact that they basically derive their distinctive meanings from the way they are semiotically contrasted in our minds with other symbols.[14] The color blue, for example, is conventionally associated with baby boys. As evident from Figure 5.2, this association can be fully understood only within the context of the essentially homologous conventional association of the color pink with baby girls [a]. The mental association of handwriting with informality, or of the French tu with intimacy, can likewise be understood only within the context of the somewhat parallel conventional association of printing with formality [b] and of vous with social distance [c]. And before we rush to the conclusion that Sunday was chosen by the Church to represent Christianity mainly because it happened to be the day of the Resurrection, we should note that, in their effort to establish their distinctiveness vis-à-vis Jews, the early Christians were primarily looking for some day other than Saturday as the pivot of their week [d].[15] (For the same reason, they later also proceeded to arrange their calendar so that Easter would never fall on the same day as the first evening of Passover.)[16]

Of course, if baby girls were all dressed in blue, baby boys could very well wear pink, as the basic structural color contrast between

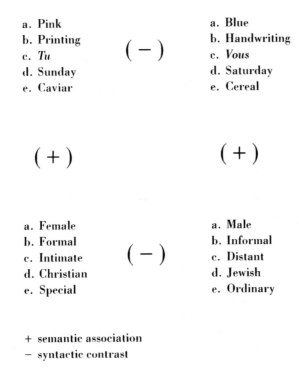

a. Pink
b. Printing
c. *Tu*
d. Sunday
e. Caviar

$(-)$

a. Blue
b. Handwriting
c. *Vous*
d. Saturday
e. Cereal

$(+)$

$(+)$

a. Female
b. Formal
c. Intimate
d. Christian
e. Special

$(-)$

a. Male
b. Informal
c. Distant
d. Jewish
e. Ordinary

+ semantic association
− syntactic contrast

Figure 5.2. The semiotic square

the sexes would still be maintained! The cultural meanings we conventionally attach to caviar and cereal [e] or to champagne and coffee[17] would likewise be completely reversed if we had the former every morning for breakfast and reserved the latter only for special occasions.

What is at stake here is a fundamental generic cultural distinction between the ordinary (the semiotically "unmarked") and the special (the semiotically "marked"). The actual contents of each of those two categories are of somewhat secondary significance.[18] Thus, for shift workers, receiving an unexpected telephone call from one's boss at home in the middle of the morning basically has the same meaning as receiving such a call in the middle of the night would for a regular daytimer.[19] By the same token, for prostitutes, kissing johns on the mouth is often considered a much more significant (and therefore dangerous) token of intimacy than fellating them. Given the semiotic role of the week as a cycle of periodic alternation between marked and unmarked time periods,[20] which particular days we choose to mark is likewise somewhat secondary. Thus, if it were Monday rather than Saturday nights that we normally reserved as "special" nights for going out, switching from seeing others on Saturday nights to Monday nights would then convey the message of becoming more, rather than less, committed to them!

Given all this, it is hardly surprising that meanings may vary from one social environment to another. Indeed, the same symbol often means different things in different social contexts (which ought to remind us, of course, that neither of those meanings is natural).

The same act or object often has different meanings in different cultures. The very existence of the Scottish kilt, for example, helps dispel the notion that skirts are inherently feminine, whereas everyday encounters among Arabs remind us that "staring" at someone is not as inherently offensive as many Americans might believe.[21] By the same token, the word *met* has quite different meanings in English and in Hebrew (where it actually means "dead").

Consider also the "language" of hair. On the Polynesian island of Tikopia, for example, men usually allow their hair to hang free on formal rather than informal occasions, certainly helping to dispel the Western notion that loose hair inherently signifies informality. The fact that on that island it is also women who cut their hair short and men who wear theirs long likewise reminds us that our conventional association of long hair with femininity is not as natural (and therefore inevitable) as we might think. Indeed, for women in Tikopia, the act of growing long hair is as symbolically defiant as the act of cutting their hair short has often been for women in the West.[22]

The fact that meanings often change considerably over time even within the same culture further underscores their unmistakably conventional nature. The Beatles' 1964 haircut, which at the time seemed so wild and disheveled, actually looked quite tame (and even short) only four years later! And although long hair seemed to be intrinsically associated in the West during the late 1960s and early 1970s with subversiveness, it certainly did not have that meaning at the time of Benjamin Franklin, Louis XIV, or Johann Sebastian Bach.

Furthermore, meanings sometimes vary considerably across contemporary cognitive subcultures within the same society. (As evident from the current cultural battles in America over the meaning of abortion, of sexual harassment, and of owning a gun, such diversity often generates discord.) Thus, for example, unlike the Christians around them, Hindus in England today clearly do not regard Easter, the cross, or the Gospels as sacred. By the same token, in the United States, whereas Jews and Muslims associate the act of eating pork with sin, neither Methodists nor Presbyterians attach any moral significance to it.

Indeed, meanings vary considerably even within the same thought community, and the same act or object can actually have very different meanings when it is socially "packaged" differently. The meaning we attach to the act of killing someone, for example, certainly changes dramatically when it happens on the battlefield rather than on the subway, and handling other people's genitals obviously means something quite different in a gynecological examination and in bed.[23] A $150 ticket for a concert likewise changes its meaning entirely when the proceeds go to AIDS victims.

By now it is probably evident that an essentialist view of symbolic meaning as an inherent property of the acts or objects with which it is conventionally associated is inadequate. It is quite clear that the "meaning" of the Finnish national anthem, for example, lies not in its actual sounds but in the mental associations they seem to evoke for some listeners *as members of a particular thought community.* In other words, if many Finns indeed respond to the symbolism of their national anthem, they certainly do so not as human beings but as Finns.

By the same token, while the sanctity of the Gospels, the Pope, or the cross is clearly not just the product of the mind of a particular individual, nor is it an inherent property of those "sacred" objects themselves.[24] Rather, it is a product of the fact that a particular thought community has chosen to sanctify them. This is obviously also true of the "virtuous" nature of chastity, the "criminal" nature of treason,[25] the "perverse" nature of bestiality, or the "noble" nature of self-sacrifice.

It is also true of the "edibility" of the things we conventionally eat. The fact that it is quite possible to eat (and even enjoy) food which we normally consider repulsive as long as we do not know exactly what it is that we are actually eating,[26] for example, shows that revulsion has more to do with our minds than with our stomachs (which should not surprise us given the fact that our vomiting center is indeed located in the brain). Yet it is obviously not just individuals' own minds. While the fact that we are usually revolted by the same food objects that many others around us also find revolting suggests that revulsion is more than just a personal response of particular individuals, the fact that those objects often vary from one culture to another clearly suggests that neither is it an entirely natural response. After all, unlike many Americans, for example, only few Japanese find raw fish revolting. Nor, for that matter, are most Frenchmen revolted by frog legs or snails.

Since neither the gastrointestinal tracts nor the vomiting centers of Frenchmen who do not find snails revolting are fundamentally different from those of Americans who do, it is quite clear that even a seemingly natural act such as vomiting is nonetheless affected by conventional, social definitions of what is repulsive. This is also true of many other seemingly natural acts such as laughing, blushing, trembling, or crying, which, in a somewhat similar fashion, are at least partly affected by unmistakably social definitions of what is "funny," "embarrassing," "dangerous,"[27] or "sad."

Thus, rather than accept the common behaviorist view of human action in terms of natural responses to stimuli, we certainly need to pay more attention to the distinctly social process of meaning attribution that, through unmistakably conventional *rules of mental association,* actually links symbolic signifiers to the particular signifieds they come to represent to us. In other words, we need to recognize the cognitive role of society as a critical mediator between reality and our minds.[28]

Meaning, in short, is an unmistakably social relation between signifier and signified. Rather than an inherent property of the symbol itself, it is a product of the particular *socio*mental connection between the symbol and the particular thought community that uses it. The meaning of symbols, thus, is a property of the way they are socially used.

Despite all this, however, we often disregard the conventional nature of symbols, thereby basically reifying them. Since their meaning is clearly not just personal (after all, it is not just a few unrelated individuals who happen to link Sunday to Christianity or who in the 1960s came to associate long hair with subversiveness), we often assume that it must therefore be natural. We thus forget that in Tunisia or Afghanistan, for example, the Finnish national anthem does not evoke any of the associations and images it so effectively evokes in Finland.

The tendency to mistake intersubjectivity for objectivity is quite evident, for example, in the way we attribute natural, "intrinsically" erotic qualities to essentially nonsexual objects such as nylon stockings, sports cars, cigarettes, and jewelry. It can also be seen in the way we sometimes confuse totemic representations of collectivities with those collectivities themselves,[29] which explains people's readiness to give their lives in order to protect their national flag as well as the

1982 war between Britain and Argentina over the barren Falkland Islands or the long-standing conflict between Arabs and Jews over Jerusalem.

Reifying the meaning of symbols basically blurs the fundamental distinction between signifier and signified, a major logical fallacy exemplified by the act of mistaking a map for the actual territory it is supposed to represent[30] or the word *rabbit* for what it happens to mean in English. As such, it denies their unmistakably conventional nature. After all, despite our fetishistic attachment to nylon stockings, their "inherent" sexiness is only a product of the minds of the advertisers who are trying to get us to buy them.[31] Nor, for that matter, is the "holy city" of Jerusalem intrinsically sacred.

The tendency to reify the meaning of symbols is eerily evocative of the highly nonreflective manner in which people process hypnotic suggestions or use language in Orwellian dystopias.[32] Sadly enough, it promotes a way of thinking that is a far cry from the remarkably sophisticated level to which human cognition has evolved since the invention of language.

The move from being able to invoke the mental image of a rabbit only by producing the actual smell of a rabbit to being able to do so by merely uttering the word *rabbit* has certainly increased our cognitive flexibility. Whereas the meaning of indicators is basically fixed, symbols can mean practically *anything*. Having a fine appreciation of their "algebraic" quality, Humpty Dumpty was indeed quite right when he told Alice: "When I use a word . . . it means just what I choose it to mean . . ."[33]

One of the most important features of strictly symbolic systems of signification such as language is the fact that, unlike clothes, for example, which have other functions besides being symbols, words are intrinsically worthless. Yet it is precisely their lack of any intrinsic meaning that allows us to attach *any* meaning we wish to them, thereby providing them with a virtually unlimited signifying potential. Indeed, "the more barren and indifferent the symbol, the greater is its semantic power."[34] The word *rabbit* can thus come to mean a doorknob, a feather, or a laptop computer if we so wish. By the same token, we can designate mere pieces of otherwise-useless paper as being worth $100 (or even thousands of dollars in the case of checks) precisely because, unlike milk or eggs, for example, money is valuable *only* as a means of exchange and is therefore intrinsically worthless![35]

Such cognitive flexibility, in fact, is one of the great advantages we have over other animals, which, being seriously constricted semiotically by the fixed meanings of the signs they use, are clearly unable to transcend their strictly indicative function. A lion cannot decide what a particular roar it produces would mean. And while dogs can certainly respond to words we teach them *(sit, stay, no)* as indicators, they obviously lack the cognitive ability to actively determine (and possibly even change) their meaning, which we, of course, are free to do with those same words *as symbols.*[36]

Reifying the meaning of symbols essentially reduces them to mere indicators and therefore implies a readiness to give up the greatest advantage that being able to use symbols offers us. It basically means trading the cognitive freedom that typically comes with flexible-mindedness[37] for the inevitably constrictive way of thinking promoted by the rigid mind. Given the virtually unlimited signifying potential of symbols, it also means a terrible waste of our distinctively human capacity to think creatively.[38]

6 /

Social Memories

Not only does our social environment influence the way we mentally process the present, it also affects the way we remember the past. Like the present, the past is to some extent also part of a social reality that, while far from being absolutely objective, nonetheless transcends our own subjectivity and is shared by others around us.

As evident from the universalistic tendency of those who study memory today to focus primarily on the formal aspects of the processes of organizing, storing, and accessing memories which we all share, they are largely interested in how *humans* remember past events. And yet, when they come to examine the actual contents of those memories, they usually go to the other extreme and focus on the individual. Nowhere is this individualistic bent more glaringly evident than in psychoanalysis, which deals almost exclusively with our distinctly personal memories.

Once again one can identify a relatively unexplored intellectual terrain made up of various "remembrance environments" lying somewhere between the strictly personal and the absolutely universal. These environments (which include, for example, the family, the workplace, the profession, the fan club, the ethnic group, the religious community, and the nation) are all larger than the individual yet at the same time considerably smaller than the entire human race.

Admittedly, there are various universal patterns of organizing, storing, and accessing past experiences that indeed characterize *all* human beings and actually distinguish human memory from that of dogs, spiders, or parrots. At the same time, it is also quite clear that we each have our own unique autobiographical memories, made up of absolutely personal experiences that we share with nobody else. Yet we also happen to have certain memories which we share with some people but not with others. Thus, for example, there are certain memories commonly shared by most Guatemalans or art historians yet only by few Australians or marine biologists. By the same token, there are many memories shared by nearly all Beatles fans, stamp collectors, or longtime readers of *Mad Magazine,* yet by no one else besides them. The unmistakably common nature of such memories indicates that they are clearly not just personal. At the same time, the fact that they are almost exclusively confined to a particular thought community shows that they are not entirely universal either.

Such memories constitute the distinctive domain of the *sociology of memory,* which, unlike any of the other cognitive sciences, focuses specifically on the social aspects of the mental act of remembering. In doing so, it certainly helps us gain a finer appreciation of the considerable extent to which our social environment affects the way we remember the past.

The work on memory typically produced by cognitive psychologists might lead one to believe that the act of remembering takes place in a social vacuum. The relative lack of explicit attention to the social context within which human memory is normally situated tends to promote a rather distorted vision of individuals as "mnemonic Robinson Crusoes" whose memories are virtually free of any social influence or constraint. Such a naive vision would be quite inappropriate even within the somewhat synthetic context of the psychological laboratory, where much of the research on memory today (with the notable exception of "ecologically" oriented work)[1] typically takes place. It is even less appropriate, however, within the context of real life.

Consider the critical role of others as witnesses whose memories help corroborate our own.[2] No wonder most courts of law do not give uncorroborated testimony the same amount of credence and official recognition as admissible evidence that they normally give to socially corroborated testimony. After all, most of us tend to feel somewhat reassured that what we seem to remember indeed happened when there are others who can verify our recollections and thereby provide them with a stamp of intersubjectivity. The terribly frustrating experience of recalling people or events that no one else seems to remember strongly resembles that of seeing things or hearing sounds which no one else does.[3]

Furthermore, there are various occasions when other people have even better access to certain parts of our past than we ourselves do and can therefore help us recall people and events which we have somehow forgotten. A wife, for example, may remind her husband about an old friend of his which he had once mentioned to her yet has since forgotten.[4] Parents, grandparents, and older siblings, of course, often remember events from our own childhood that we cannot possibly recall. In fact, many of our earliest "memories" are actually recollections of stories we heard from them about our childhood.[5] In an odd way, they remember them for us!

Yet such social mediation can also assume a somewhat negative form, since such "mnemonic others" can also help block our access to certain events in our own past, to the point of actually preventing some of them from becoming memories in the first place! This is particularly critical in the case of very young children, who still depend on others around them to define what is real (as well as "memorable") and what is not. A 35-year-old secretary whose boss tells her to "forget this ever happened" will probably be psychologically independent enough to store that forbidden memory in her mind anyway. However, a five-year-old boy whose mother flatly denies that a certain event they have just experienced together ever took place will most likely have a much harder time resisting her pressure to suppress it from his consciousness and may thus end up repressing it altogether.

Such instances remind us, of course, that the reasons we sometimes tend to repress our memories may not always be internal and that our social environment certainly plays a major role in helping us determine what is "memorable" and what we can (or even should) forget. Needless to say, they further demonstrate the ubiquity of sociomental control.

The notion that there are certain things that one *should* forget also underscores the normative dimension of memory, which is typically ignored by cognitive psychology. Like the curricular institutionalization of required history classes in school, it reminds us that remembering is more than just a spontaneous personal act, as it also happens to be regulated by unmistakably social *rules of remembrance* that tell us quite specifically what we should remember and what we must forget.

Such rules often determine how far back we remember. In the same way that society helps delineate the scope of our attention and concern through various norms of focusing, it also manages to affect the extent of our mental reach into the past by setting certain historical horizons beyond which past events are regarded as somehow irrelevant and, as such, often forgotten altogether.[6]

The way society affects the "depth" of individuals' memory by relegating certain parts of the past to official oblivion is often quite explicit, as in the case of the 1990 ruling by the Israeli broadcasting authorities prohibiting television and radio announcers from referring to places in present-day Israel by their old Arab names. Just as blatant is the aptly-named statute of limitations, the ultimate institutionalization of the idea that it is actually possible to put certain things "behind us." The very notion of such a statute implies that even events that we all agree happened can nonetheless be mentally banished to a "pre-historical" past that is considered legally irrelevant, and thereby officially forgotten. The unmistakably conventional nature of any statute of limitations, of course, reminds us that it is very often society that determines which particular bygones we let be bygones.

Yet the extent to which our social environment affects the "depth" of our memory is also manifested somewhat more tacitly in the way we conventionally begin historical narratives.[7] By defining a certain moment in history as the actual beginning of a particular historical narrative, it implicitly defines for us everything that preceded that moment as mere "pre-history" which we can practically forget. Thus, for example, when the founders of Islam established the flight of the Prophet from Mecca to Medina in A.D. 622 as the pivot of the conventional Mohammedan chronological dating system, they implicitly defined everything that had ever happened prior to that momentous event as a mere prelude to the "real" history that every Muslim ought to remember.[8] By the same token, when sociologists say (as they often do) that sociology was "born" in the 1830s with the work of Auguste Comte (who was indeed the first ever to use the term "sociology"), they are implicitly saying that their students need not really read the work of Aristotle, Hobbes, or Rousseau, which is somehow only "pre-sociological."[9]

Nowhere is the unmistakably social partitioning of the past into a memorable "history" and a practically forgettable "pre-history" more glaringly evident than in the case of so-called discoveries. When the *New York Times,* for example, offers its readers a brief historical profile of Mozambique that begins with its "discovery" by the Portuguese in 1498 and fails to remind them that that particular moment marks only the beginning of the *European* chapter in its history, it relegates that country's entire pre-European past to official oblivion. A similar example of such "mnemonic decapitation" is the way Icelanders begin the official history of their island. Both the Book of Settlements *(Landnámabók)* and Book of Icelanders *(Íslendingabók)* mention in passing the fact that when the first

Norwegians arrived on the island in the ninth century, they found Irish monks already living there, yet their commitment to Iceland's Scandinavian identity (and therefore origins) leads them to present those Norwegians as its *first* settlers![10] While not trying to explicitly conceal the actual presence of Celts prior to Iceland's official "discovery" by Scandinavians, they nevertheless treat them as irrelevant to its "real" history.

Consider also the way we conventionally regard Columbus's first encounter with America as its official "discovery," thereby suppressing the memory of the millions of native Americans who were already living there. The notion that Columbus "discovered" America goes hand in hand with the idea that American history begins only in 1492 and that all events in the Western Hemisphere prior to that year are just part of its "pre-American" past. From this historiographic perspective, nothing that predates 1492 truly belongs in "American history." Indeed, it is conventionally considered part of a mere "pre-Columbian" prologue.

America's "pre-history" includes not only its own native past but also earlier, "pre-Columbian" European encounters with it, which explains why the Norse voyages across the Atlantic (to Greenland, Newfoundland, and possibly Nova Scotia) in the late tenth and early eleventh centuries are still not considered part of the official narrative of "the discovery of America."[11] Despite the fact that most of us are fully aware of the indisputable Norse presence on the western shores of the Atlantic almost five centuries before Columbus, we still regard his 1492 landfall in the Bahamas as the official beginning of American history. After all, if "America" was indeed born only on October 12, 1492 (a notion implicitly supported by the official annual celebration of its "birthday" on Columbus Day), nothing that had happened there prior to that date can be considered truly part of "American history."[12]

Needless to say, this grand division of the past into a memorable "history" and an officially forgettable "pre-history" is neither logical nor natural. It is an unmistakably social, normative convention. One needs to be socialized to view Columbus's first voyage to the Caribbean as the beginning of American history. One certainly needs to be taught to regard everything that had ever happened in America prior to 1492 as a mere prelude to its "real" history. Only then, indeed, can one officially forget "pre-Columbian" America.

We usually learn what we should remember and what we can forget as part of our *mnemonic socialization,* a process that normally takes place when we enter an altogether new social environment, such as when we get married, start a new job, convert to another religion, or emigrate to another country.[13] (It is a subtle process that usually happens rather tacitly: listening to a family member recount a shared experience, for example, implicitly teaches one what is considered memorable and what one can actually forget.) In acquainting us with the specific rules of remembrance that operate in that environment, it introduces us to a particular "tradition" of remembering.

A *mnemonic tradition* includes not only what we come to remember as members of a particular thought community but also *how* we remember it. After all, much of what we seem to "remember" is actually filtered (and often inevitably distorted) through a process of subsequent interpretation, which affects not only the actual facts we recall but also the particular "light" in which we happen to recall them. Thus, it is hardly surprising that a girl who grows up in a highly traditionalistic family which tends to embellish and romanticize the past would come to "remember" her great-grandfather as a larger-than-life, almost mythical figure. Indeed, that is why Americans who grow up today in liberal and conservative homes "remember" so differently the great social upheavals of the 1960s and 1970s.

As the very first social environment in which we learn to interpret our own experience, the family plays a critical role in our mnemonic socialization. In fact, most subsequent interpretations of early "recollections" of particular events in one's life are only *rei*nterpretations of the way they were originally experienced *and remembered* within the context of one's family! That explains why we often spend a lot of mental effort as we grow up trying to "reclaim" our own personal recollections from our parents or older siblings. Indeed, what is often experienced in intensive psychotherapy is the almost inevitable clash between recalling certain people and events through the *mnemonic lenses* provided by our immediate family and recalling those same people and events by gradually regaining contact with deeper layers of our selves.

Yet mnemonic traditions affect our memory even more significantly by prompting us to adopt a particular cognitive "bias"[14] that leads us to remember certain things but not others. As an increasing body of research on memory seems to indicate, familiarity usually breeds memorability, as we tend to remember information that we can somehow fit into ready-made, familiar schematic mental structures that "make sense" to us[15] (the same structures that, as we have already seen, affect the way we mentally process our perceptual experience). That is why it is usually much easier to recall that a particular character in a story we have read happened to wear glasses when she is a librarian, for example, than when she is a waitress or a nurse. This tendency to remember things schematically applies not only to actual facts but also to the way we recall the general "gist" of events (which is often all we can remember of them)[16] as well as to the way we interpret those memories.[17]

To further appreciate such tendency to remember events that proceed according to a certain schematic set of prior expectations, consider also the formulaic, script-like "plot structures"[18] we often use to narrate the past, a classic example of which is the traditional Zionist view of the history of Jews' "exilic" life outside the Land of Israel almost exclusively in terms of persecution and victimization.[19] I find it quite interesting, in this regard, that only in my late thirties did I first realize that Captain Alfred Dreyfus, who I had always "remembered" languishing in the penal colony on Devil's Island *until he died* (following the infamous 1894 trial at which he was wrongly convicted for treason against France), was actually exonerated by the French authorities and even decorated with the Legion of Honor twelve years later! Having grown up in Israel during the 1950s and having been socialized into the Zionist mnemonic tradition of narrating European Jewish history, it is hardly surprising that that is how I "remembered" the end of the famous Dreyfus Affair.

Needless to say, the schematic mental structures on which mnemonic traditions typically rest are neither "logical" nor natural. Most of them are either culture-specific or subculture-specific,[20] and therefore something we acquire as part of our mnemonic socialization. Thus, if we tend to remember so much better situational details that are salient in our own culture or subculture,[21] it is mostly because so many of our pre-existing expectations are based on conventionalized, social typifications.[22]

Once again we are seeing indisputable evidence of society's ubiquitous cognitive role as a mediator between individuals and their own experience. In fact, since most of the schematic mental structures that help us organize and access our memories are part of our unmistakably social "stock of knowledge,"[23] much of what we seem to recall is only socially, rather than personally, familiar to us! Indeed, it is what we come to "remember" *as members of particular thought communities.*

The fact that I can actually "recall" the Dreyfus Affair also reminds us that what we remember includes far more than just what we have personally experienced. In other words, it underscores the unmistakably impersonal aspect of memory.

I was already forty-three when I first saw Venice, yet I soon realized that it was actually quite familiar to me. The majestic Grand Canal, for example, was something I had already "seen" on the cover of an album of brass concerti by Venetian composer Antonio Vivaldi when I was eighteen. And when I saw the infamous "Lion's Mouth" (where anonymous accusers once dropped their denunciations of fellow Venetians to the secret police) in the Palace of the Doges, I was actually seeing something I remembered from a book I had read some twenty years earlier.

Stored in my mind are rather vivid "recollections" of my great-grandfather (who I never even met and about whom I know only indirectly from my mother's, grandmother's, and great-aunt's accounts), the Crucifixion (the way I first "saw" it in Nicholas Ray's film *The King of Kings* when I was twelve), and the first voyage around the world (the way I first envisioned it when I read Stefan Zweig's biography of Ferdinand Magellan as a teenager). I have somewhat similar "memories" of the Inca Empire, the Punic Wars, and Genghis Khan, despite the fact that I personally experienced none of them.

In fact, neither are my recollections of most of the "historical" events that have taken place in my own lifetime entirely personal.[24] What I usually remember of those events is how they were described by others who did experience them personally! They are socially mediated memories that are based entirely on secondhand accounts of others.[25] Thus, for example, I "remember" the French pullout from Algeria and the Soviet invasion of Prague mainly through the way they were reported at the time in the newspapers. I likewise "recall" the Eichmann trial, the Cuban missile crisis, and the landing of Apollo 11 on the moon mainly through radio and television reports.[26]

In fact, much of what we seem to "remember" we did not actually experience personally. We only do so as members of particular families, organizations, nations, and other *mnemonic communities*[27] to which we happen to belong. Thus, for example, it is mainly as a Jew that I "recall" so vividly the Babylonian destruction of the First Temple in Jerusalem more than twenty-five centuries before I was born. By the same token, it is as a member of my family that I "remember" my great-great-grandmother (whose memory is probably no longer carried by anyone outside it), and as a soccer fan that I recall Uruguay's historic winning goal against Brazil in the 1950 World Cup

final. Consider also the special place of the Stonewall riots and of Charlie Parker's early gigs with Dizzy Gillespie at Minton's Play House in the respective memories of homosexuals and jazz aficionados. Indeed, being social presupposes the ability to experience events that happened to groups and communities long before we even joined them as if they were somehow part of our own past, an ability so perfectly captured by the traditional Jewish claim, explicitly repeated every Passover, that "we were slaves to Pharaoh in Egypt, and God brought us out of there with a mighty hand." (On Passover Jews also recite the following passage from the Haggadah: "In every generation, a man should see himself as though he had gone forth from Egypt. As it is said: 'And you shall tell your son on that day, it is because of what God did for me when I went forth from Egypt.'")[28] Such existential fusion of one's own biography with the history of the groups or communities to which one belongs is an indispensable part of one's unmistakably social identity as an anthropologist, a Mormon, a Native American, a Miami Dolphins fan, or a member of the U.S. Marine Corps.

In marked contrast to our strictly autobiographical memory, such *sociobiographical memory*[29] also accounts for the sense of pride, pain, or shame we sometimes experience as a result of things that happened to groups and communities to which we belong long before we even joined them.[30] Consider the national pride of present-day Greeks, much of which rests on the glorious accomplishments of fellow Greek scholars, artists, and philosophers some twenty-four centuries ago, or the institutional arrogance of many current faculty of academic departments that were considered great forty years ago but have since been in decline. Consider also the long tradition of pain and suffering carried by many present-day American descendants of nineteenth-century African slaves, or the great sense of shame that pervades the experience of many young Germans born many years after the collapse of the Nazi regime.

Indeed, identifying with a particular collective past is an important part of the process of acquiring a particular social identity

(hence the appeal for some students of African-American and Women's Studies programs in universities, for example). Familiarizing new members with their collective past is an important part of groups' and communities' general efforts to incorporate them. Business corporations, colleges, and army battalions, for example, often introduce new members to their collective history as part of their general "orientation." Children whose parents came to the United States from Ghana, Ecuador, or Cambodia are likewise taught in school to "remember" Paul Revere and the *Mayflower* as part of their own past. From Poland to Mexico, from Israel to Taiwan, the study of national history plays a major role in the general effort of the modern state to foster a national identity.[31]

At the same time (and for precisely the same reasons), exiting a group or a community typically involves forgetting its past. Children who are abandoned by one of their parents, for example, rarely carry on the memories of his or her family. Children of assimilated immigrants likewise rarely learn much from their parents about the history of the societies they chose to leave, both physically and psychologically, behind them.

Given its highly impersonal nature, social memory need not even be stored in individuals' minds. Indeed, there are some unmistakably impersonal "sites"[32] of memory.

It was the invention of language that first freed human memory from the need to be stored in individuals' minds. As soon as it became technically possible for people to somehow "share" their personal experiences with others, those experiences were no longer exclusively theirs and could therefore be preserved as somewhat impersonal recollections even after they themselves were long gone. In fact, with language, memories can actually pass from one person to another even when there is no direct contact between them, through an intermediate. Indeed, that has always been one of the main social functions of the elderly, who, as the de facto custodians of the social memories of their communities, have traditionally

served as "mnemonic go-betweens," essentially linking historically separate generations who would otherwise never be able to mentally "connect" with one another.

Such "mnemonic transitivity" allows for the social preservation of memories in stories, poems, and legends that are transmitted from one generation to the next. One finds such oral traditions[33] in practically any social community—from families, churches, law firms, and college fraternities to ethnic groups, air force bases, basketball teams, and radio stations. It was thus an oral tradition that enabled the Marranos in Spain, for example, to preserve their secret Jewish heritage (and therefore identity) for so many generations. It was likewise through stories that the memory of their spectacular eleventh-century encounter with America was originally preserved by Icelanders, more than a century before it was first recorded in their famous sagas and some 950 years before it was first corroborated by actual archaeological finds in Newfoundland.[34]

Furthermore, ever since the invention of writing several thousand years ago, it is also possible to actually bypass any oral contact, however indirect, between the original carrier of a particular recollection and its various future retrievers. Present-day readers of Saint Augustine's *Confessions* can actually "share" his personal recollections of his youth despite the fact that he has already been dead for more than fifteen centuries! Doctors can likewise share patient histories readily, since the highly impersonal clinical memories captured in their records are accessible even when those who originally recorded them there are not readily available for immediate consultation.[35] That explains the tremendous significance of documents in science (laboratory notes, published results of research), law (affidavits, contracts), diplomacy (telegrams, treaties), business (receipts, signed agreements), and bureaucracy (letters of acceptance, minutes of meetings), as well as of the archives, libraries, and computer files where they are typically stored.[36] It also accounts for the critical role of history textbooks in the mnemonic socialization of present and future generations.

Yet preserving social memories requires neither oral nor written transmission. Given the inherent durability of material objects as well as the fact that they are mnemonically evocative in an immediate, "tangible" manner, they too play an important role in helping us retain memories.[37] Hence the role of ruins, relics, and old buildings as *social souvenirs*. A visit to the National Museum of Anthropology in Mexico City, for example, helps "connect" modern Mexican "pilgrims" to their Toltec, Maya, and Aztec origins. A walk through the old neighborhoods of Jerusalem likewise allows present-day Jews a quasi-personal "contact" with their collective past.[38]

As evident from the modern advent of preservationism[39] as well as from the modern state's political use of archaeology as part of its general effort to promote nationalism,[40] we are certainly more than just passive consumers of such quasi-physical mnemonic links to our collective past. Numerous medals, plaques, tombstones, war memorials, Halls of Fame, and other commemorative monuments (and the fact that we make them from stone or metal rather than paper or wood)[41] serve as evidence that we purposefully design such future sites of memory well in advance. Like souvenirs, class yearbooks, and antiques,[42] such objects have a purely commemorative value for us, and we design them strictly for the purpose of allowing future generations mnemonic access to their collective past.[43] The entire meaning of such "pre-ruins" derives from the fact that they are mnemonically evocative and will therefore help us in the future to recover our past.

The self-conscious effort to preserve the past for posterity is manifested even more poignantly in the statues, portraits, stamps, coins, and paper money we produce as social souvenirs. The visual images so vividly captured on them represent an ambitious attempt to somehow "freeze" time and allow future generations the fullest possible mnemonic access to major individuals and events from their collective past. National galleries that try to offer posterity a comprehensive visual encapsulation of a nation's history (the collection of paintings displayed in the U.S. Capitol building,[44] Diego Rivera's murals at the National Palace in Mexico City) are the culmination of such artistic endeavors.

Since the invention of the camera (as well as its two major offspring, the motion-picture and television cameras), these more traditional means of "capturing" the past have gradually given way to photographs and films.[45] The family photo album and the television archive, indeed, are among the major modern sites of social memory. In fact, it is primarily through snapshots, home movies, and television footage that most of us nowadays remember old relatives, family weddings, or the Gulf War.

As evident from the rapid evolution of audio-recording technology from the phonograph to the portable cassette-recorder, in our attempt to somehow "freeze" time we actually try to capture not only visual images but also the very sounds of the past. Historic recordings of Winston Churchill's speeches and Vladimir Horowitz's concerts, for example, underscore the growing significance of tapes, cassettes, and compact discs as modern sites of social memory.

Video technology, of course, represents the modern attempt to integrate such graphic and sonic efforts to preserve the past. The ultimate progeny of the camera and the phonograph, the camcorder generates remarkably vivid audio-visual memories that are virtually independent of any individual carrier! The famous videotaped beating of Rodney King by members of the Los Angeles police, for example, is the epitome of such absolutely disembodied and therefore truly impersonal memory. As evident from its repeated use in court, it may very well represent (not unlike the increasingly common use of instant video replay in televised sports)[46] the ultimate victory of social and therefore "official" over purely personal memory.

Not only are many of our recollections impersonal, they are often also collective. My memory of the first mile ever run under four minutes, for example, is actually shared by the entire track world. So are some of the memories I share with other sociologists, Jews, or Rutgers University employees. In each of these cases my own recollections are part of a *collective memory*[47] shared by an entire community as a whole.

The collective memory of a mnemonic community is quite different from the sum total of the personal recollections of its various individual members,[48] as it includes only those that are *commonly shared* by all of them (in the same way that public opinion, for example, is more than just an aggregate of individuals' personal opinions).[49] In other words, it involves the integration of various different personal pasts into a single common past that all members of a community come to remember collectively. America's collective memory of the Vietnam War, for example, is thus more than just an aggregate of all the war-related recollections of individual Americans, just as Israel's collective memory of the Holocaust[50] is more than the mere sum of the personal recollections of all the Holocaust survivors living in Israel.

We must be particularly careful not to mistake personalized manifestations of a mnemonic community's collective memory for genuinely personal recollections.[51] When asked to list the first names that come to their minds in response to the prompt "American history from its beginning through the end of the Civil War," Americans usually list the same people—George Washington, Abraham Lincoln, Thomas Jefferson, Benjamin Franklin, Robert E. Lee, John Adams, and Ulysses S. Grant.[52] The fact that so many different individuals happen to have the same "free" associations about their nation's past shows that their memories are not as independent as we might think but merely personalized manifestations of a single common collective memory. In so doing, it also underscores the tremendous significance of mnemonic socialization.

Yet the notion of a "collective memory" implies a past that is not only commonly shared but also jointly remembered (that is, "co-memorated"). By helping ensure that an entire mnemonic community will come to remember its past *together,* as a group, society affects not only what and who we remember but also when we remember it!

Commemorative anniversaries such as the 1992 Columbus quincentennial, the 1995 fiftieth anniversary of the end of World War II, and the 1976 American bicentennial are classic manifestations of such *mnemonic synchronization.* Yet we also "co-remember" past events by associating them with holidays and other "memorial days" which we jointly celebrate on a regular annual[53] (or even weekly, as in the case of both the Sabbath and the Lord's Day)[54] basis. Fixed in a mnemonic community's calendar, such days ensure members' synchronized access to their collective past. Indeed, keeping certain past events in our collective memory by ensuring their annual commemoration is one of the main functions of the calendar.[55]

Thus, on Easter, millions of Christians come to remember their common spiritual origins together, as a community. By the same token, every Passover, Jews all over the world jointly remember their collective birth as a people. The annual commemoration of the French Revolution on Bastille Day and of the European colonization of New England on Thanksgiving Day play similar "co-evocative" roles for Frenchmen and Americans, respectively.

That also explains various attempts throughout history to remove certain holidays from the calendar in an effort to obliterate the collective memories they evoke. The calendrical dissociation of Easter from Passover, for example, was thus part of a conscious effort by the Church to "decontaminate" Christians' collective memory from somewhat embarrassing Jewish elements,[56] whereas the calendar of the French Revolution represented an attempt to establish a mnemonically sanitized secular holiday cycle that would be devoid of any Christian memories.[57] Given all this, it is also clear why the recent political battle over the inclusion of Martin Luther King Jr.'s birthday in the American calendar was actually a battle over the place of African Americans in America's collective memory.

———

The battle over whether to officially include Martin Luther King Jr.'s birthday in the American calendar is one of numerous battles fought between as well as within mnemonic communities over the social legacy of the past. The very existence of such *mnemonic battles* further underscores the social dimension of human memory.

The most common mnemonic battles are the ones fought over the "correct" way to interpret the past. As we develop a collective sense of history, we may not always agree on how a particular historical figure or event ought to be remembered. While many Americans regard Columbus as a hero who embodies the modern Western quest for knowledge and spirit of free enterprise, there are many others who claim that he should actually be remembered as the villainous spearhead of the modern Western expansionist spirit that is responsible for both colonialism and the massive destruction of the environment.[58] By the same token, whereas many Israelis still accept the official Zionist view of the fall of Masada and the Bar-Kokhba rebellion nineteen centuries ago as exemplary heroic events, a growing number of others are voicing the concern that they are actually symptomatic of a rather myopic stubbornness that resulted in terrible national disasters that could have been avoided by a more politically expedient way of dealing with the Romans who occupied Judaea.[59] Consider also the cultural battles fought among Americans over the "correct" interpretation of Watergate,[60] or the debate among historians over whether the origins of Greek (and therefore Western) civilization are Indo-European or African,[61] as well as everyday marital battles over past infidelities.

Mnemonic battles are also fought over what ought to be collectively remembered in the first place. Eurocentrists, multiculturalists, and feminists, among others, battle over the literary tradition into which young members of society ought to be mnemonically socialized. Consider also the problem of delineating the historical narratives that are to be remembered. Given the inherently conventional nature of any beginning,[62] "where" a particular historical narrative ought to begin is by no means self-evident.[63] After all, even people who are trying to recount an event they have just witnessed together often disagree on the precise point at which their account ought to begin. It is not at all clear, for example, whether we should begin the "story" of the Vietnam War during the Johnson or Kennedy years. Nor is it absolutely clear whether the narrative of the events leading to the Gulf War ought to begin in August 1990, when Iraq invaded Kuwait (which is the standard American version), or several decades earlier, when both were still part of a single, undivided political entity (which is the standard Iraqi version).

As we might expect, such narratological pluralism often generates discord. Japan and the United States wage an ongoing mnemonic battle over the inclusion of the Japanese attack on Pearl Harbor in 1941 in the narrative of the events leading to the atomic bombings of Hiroshima and Nagasaki by the United States four years later. Consider also the Arab-Israeli dispute over the point at which a fair narration of the history of the West Bank ought to begin, or the strong objection of Native Americans to the Eurocentric depiction of 1492 as the beginning of American history. After all, for anyone whose ancestors lived in America thousands of years before it was "discovered" by Europe, that date certainly constitutes more of an ending than a beginning.

Like Akira Kurosawa's *Rashomon*, the fact that such discord exists at all reminds us that our memory of the past is not entirely objective, since we evidently do not all remember it the same way. Yet mnemonic battles usually involve not just individuals but entire communities, and are typically fought in the public arena (such as in newspaper editorials and radio talk shows), which suggests that the past is not entirely subjective either. That remembering is more than just a personal act is also evident from the fact that major changes in the way we view the past (such as our growing sensitivity to multiculturalist historiographic concerns) usually correspond to major social changes that affect entire mnemonic communities.[64] This, again, underscores the intersubjective, unmistakably social dimension of human memory.

7 /

Standard Time

Not only the content of our memories but also the way we mentally "place" them in the past is affected by our social environment, as evident from the way that we so often use unmistakably impersonal temporal reference frameworks[1] for dating even absolutely personal events in our own past. I thus recall having fractured my elbow "in 1985," for example, or having my house painted "just before the Gulf War."

Admittedly, we often date the occurrence of past events in terms of strictly personal dating frameworks used only by ourselves, as when I remember something as having taken place "250,000 cigarettes ago" or "3,000 quarts of booze ago"[2] or around the time I discovered chamber music. These are all instances of a strictly personal manner of dating that is absolutely meaningless to anyone other than the person using it. Yet we also happen to date past events in unmistakably impersonal, intersubjective terms that are meaningful to others beside us as well. Thus, when couples recall something as having occurred on their second date, a week before they moved to San Francisco, or the year they bought their Chevy, for example, they are actually using *social dating frameworks* based on temporal landmarks derived from their collective life as a couple. So do college professors who date past departmental events in terms such as "a couple of years before we hired Gordon," "on Carol's first semester as chair," or "the year Nick came up for tenure."

The standard chronological "eras" we use for (formally as well as informally) dating past events likewise revolve around essentially impersonal, collectively significant temporal milestones.[3] The birth of Christ (for Christians) and the flight of Mohammed from Mecca to Medina in A.D. 622 (for Muslims) are classic examples of such *sociotemporal landmarks.* So, for that matter, are the wars, revolutions, and various calamities (earthquakes, hurricanes, droughts, fires, epidemics)[4] we often use as temporal anchors for dating even strictly personal events in our past.

Unlike the last time one had one's period or changed the oil filter in one's car, such events are the foundations of unmistakably impersonal dating frameworks used not only by specific individuals but also by entire mnemonic communities. Thus, for example, when I mention in a lecture that something happened "in 1628," my entire audience is jointly transported mentally to the very same point in history. It is such frameworks that make it possible to integrate several different personal pasts into a single common past. Indeed, with the Christian Era having attained practically universal status (after all, the date "1628" has the exact same chronological meaning in Switzerland, Costa Rica, and Angola),[5] such a past is increasingly becoming a global one as well.

Yet it is not only the past that we date in an intersubjective, social manner, but the future and the present as well.

The way we date future events is, again, partly personal, as when we plan to take a shower, make a particular telephone call, or get married in such terms as "soon," "later," or "someday." Yet it is also partly social, as when we start training for "the 2004 Olympics," plan a vacation for "August," or schedule an appointment for "next Thursday at 6:00." By the same token, when an anorectic patient is told by her doctor that she will be discharged from the hospital as soon as she weighs one hundred pounds, they both situate that moment in a single, *common* future.[6] So do a professor and a student who plan to meet as soon as a paper on which the latter is currently working is completed.

The unmistakably social nature of the manner in which we mentally "place" events in time is also evident from the way we "date" the present. Admittedly, we often "date" the present in strictly personal terms such as the number of college credits we have already completed, the number of the page we are on in the book we are currently reading, or the number of onions we still have to peel and slice for the soup we are making. Yet we also do it in standard terms that are shared by others beside us as well—"a quarter to seven," "Saturday," "August 20," "two games before the end of the season," "three weeks before the Illinois primaries," and so on. (We usually "date" the present either in terms of our temporal distance from a specific historical landmark or by "anchoring" it within a standard calendrical cycle such as the day, the week, the month, or the year.)

Doing this implies being able to convert strictly personal forms of time reckoning into standard temporal designations that have the exact same meaning for everyone using them. Such integration of various different personal "times" into a single *common time* (made up of a common past, a common present,[7] and a common future) presupposes unmistakably impersonal, *standard time-reckoning frameworks* such as clock time and the calendar. In other words, it presupposes a standard language of reckoning time in which one says "next Thursday at seven" rather than "soon" and "in 1506" instead of "long ago," a language that allows us to agree that it is now "11:25" and that today is "Wednesday, November 26, 1997."

Standardizing the way we reckon time is a necessary prerequisite for participation in a world that is also shared by others beside us. It is at the basis of any effort to coordinate human action at the level of families, organizations,[8] communities,[9] or entire societies. Even a simple act such as making an appointment with someone would be practically impossible without it!

Standard time is one of the pillars of the intersubjective, social world. Indeed, social life would not have been possible were it not for our ability to reckon time in a standard, common fashion. If we "did not have a homogeneous conception of time . . . all consensus among minds, and thus all common life, would become impossible."[10]

Given all this, it is hardly surprising that not knowing what day of the week or what year it is is often regarded as indicative of some serious socio-clinical problem, as evident from some of the routine questions typically asked during psychiatric evaluation. People who do not use standard time clearly do not inhabit the same phenomenal world shared by those around them. They are confined to their own inner worlds and cannot "enter" the intersubjective, social world.[11]

It is the anxiety about being barred from mental participation in the social world that accounts for the somewhat uneasy feeling that usually accompanies the realization that our watch is standing still or that we cannot recall what day it is,[12] a rather disorienting experience that strongly resembles that of waking from a deep sleep.[13] It is the dreadful prospect of "mental exile" from the social world that explains why castaway sailors and prisoners in solitary confinement would try to keep count of the days of the week even when they are all by themselves, far away from human civilization.[14] And when Leo Tolstoy's Ivan Ilych does not seem to care whether it is Friday or Sunday,[15] he is obviously dying, since the living would rarely risk ignoring standard time.

Being "sociotemporally disoriented" is a rather common experience during vacations, when we are somewhat less compulsive about wearing a watch and often lose count of the days of the week.[16] Yet even on such occasions rarely ever are we truly free from the temporal grip of our social environment. Even vacationers need to know what day or time it is to avoid going to museums on the days they are closed, being late for breakfast, or missing their return flight home.

This is why getting one's first watch is often regarded as a ritual of practical as well as symbolic initiation into the social world of adults. Wearing this portable, miniature version of the town-square tower clock[17] greatly facilitates our mental participation in a world commonly shared by others beside us. Even when I am alone, a tiny machine attached to my arm nevertheless connects me to others in my social milieu![18]

In fact, along with the Gregorian Calendar, the Christian Era, and the seven-day week, clock time is part of what is nowadays becoming an essentially global time-reckoning system.[19] After all, 1996 was 1996 in Armenia as well as in Peru, and when it is Sunday in Cape Town it is also Sunday in both Damascus and Madrid. (By the same token, when it is November 26 in Dublin it is also November 26 in both Tunis and Prague.) And though the possibility that it would be midnight at the same moment all over the world is obviously precluded by the spherical shape of the earth, the fact that when it is 8:56 A.M. in Rio de Janeiro it is exactly 3:56 A.M. in Vancouver and 1:56 P.M. in Tel Aviv suggests that people around the globe use the same standard time-reckoning system.

Yet the almost-universal status of this system does not mean that it is therefore also a natural one. Just because we all happen to use clock time, the Gregorian calendar, and the seven-day week, for example, does not mean that we should therefore also reify their existence. Based on unmistakably *socio*temporal arrangements,[20] they are certainly not as natural as they may appear to us at first glance.

The introduction of standard clock time, for example, marks a most significant turn away from reckoning time in accordance with nature and its cycles. Since we no longer set our clocks and watches by the sun, as we once did, the time they indicate is far less grounded in nature (and therefore also less inevitable). After all, within each of the standard "time zones" we have been using for the past 115 years,[21] there is only one meridian where clock time actually corresponds to solar time (so that 12:00 P.M. indeed marks the exact moment when the sun reaches its zenith). With the exception of that single meridian, there is always at least some discrepancy between the two. Indeed, in communities that are located seven and a half degrees of longitude east or west of that meridian, clock time may differ by as much as thirty minutes from solar time. (Since the earth completes a full rotation on its axis every twenty-four hours, actual solar time varies by four minutes for every degree of longitude.)

To further appreciate the unmistakably conventional nature of clock time, consider also the existing one-hour time differentials between neighboring time zones. With standard time, we have managed to establish mathematically elegant, rounded off clock-time differentials between almost any two points around the globe. (In the few exceptional cases when the existing clock-time differential is not an exact number of hours, it is nonetheless designated in terms of a certain number of hours and thirty [as in the cases of Iran, Afghanistan, India, or Newfoundland] or forty-five [as in the cases of Guyana and Nepal] minutes from Greenwich Mean Time.)[22] And yet, in marked contrast to the awkward though honest solar-time differentials (such as thirty-eight minutes and twenty-six and a quarter seconds) that actually exist between almost any two points on earth, such mathematically "neat" clock-time differentials are inaccurate from a purely physiotemporal (and thus natural) standpoint. That is also true of the abrupt one-hour clock-time differentials often created by time-zone boundaries between communities that are actually within walking distance of each other.

The differences between clock time and solar time are further complicated by the way we actually divide the world into time zones. Each country can practically choose its own standard (or standards) of time, which creates many situations that, while politically (and thus sociotemporally) understandable, are nonetheless quite awkward from a strictly physiotemporal standpoint. Thus, as a result of the fact that China, which is about as wide as the United States, chooses to squeeze what could be four different time zones into a single one, the standard time for western Tibet is two and a half hours ahead of that for Calcutta in neighboring India, despite the physiotemporally embarrassing fact that it is about half an hour *behind* it in actual solar time![23] (In a similar vein, as a result of the particular way in which the boundary between the Pacific and Mountain time zones happens to cut across North America, one has to move one's watch one hour forward when one travels from Las Vegas to Boise despite the fact that one is actually traveling westward rather than eastward.) By the same token, when it is 9:20 A.M. along most of Argentina's western border, it is still only 7:20 in the southeastern provinces of Colombia, which lie exactly on the same meridian. Even more striking is the twenty-four-hour clock-time differential between the islands of Tonga and Midway (which are actually only two degrees of longitude away from each other), the obvious result of the particular way in which the International Date Line happens to zigzag the Pacific.

Consider also, in this regard, the unmistakably conventional common practice of advancing standard clock time by an hour for part of the year. While it may seem quite natural (and therefore inevitable) given the seasonal differences in the length of daylight, the idea of introducing daylight saving time was a social decision. Furthermore, even when we make a conscious effort to be physiotemporally sensitive and accommodate nature and its rhythms, we nevertheless end up choosing to advance standard clock time by an unmistakably conventional sociotemporal interval.

The other main constituents of our standard time-reckoning system are just as conventional as clock time. Despite our common tendency to reify them, they all represent unmistakably sociotemporal (rather than strictly physiotemporal or biotemporal) arrangements and are therefore by no means inevitable.

Consider, for example, the hour, the minute, and the second. As fractions of the day, they are essentially mathematical (and therefore absolutely artificial) cycles that do not correspond to any natural periodicity. Nor, for that matter, does the week, which represents the boldest human effort to calendrically ignore nature altogether.[24]

The other major standard cycles we use for reckoning the time are, likewise, only rough approximations of the actual natural periodicities to which they correspond. As such, they are certainly not as inevitable as they may seem to us at first glance.

Even the day, arguably the most natural of the cycles that constitute our standard system of reckoning the time, does not always correspond to the actual period of a full rotation of the earth on its axis. After all, there are two calendar days every year that are not twenty-four, but twenty-three (the day on which we get on daylight saving time) or twenty-five (the day on which we get off daylight saving time), hours long.

The calendar year, another pillar of our standard system of reckoning the time, is also a rough approximation of the actual 365 days, 5 hours, 48 minutes, and 46 seconds it takes the earth to complete a full revolution around the sun. Though it is obviously much more convenient mathematically, being a precise multiple of the day, it nonetheless distorts the actual physiotemporal relations between the earth and the sun. Indeed, it is in order to somehow make up for these nearly six hours which we omit from our calendar every year that we add an extra 366th day every four years at the end of February.

Mathematical convenience alone also accounts for the fact that we add an extra day every four years rather than six extra hours every year, as well as for the fact that it is a full twenty-four-hour day rather than the actual extra twenty-three hours, fifteen minutes, and four seconds that accumulate every four years. While certainly more convenient from a strictly mathematical standpoint, such a calendrical arrangement creates a physiotemporal distortion which indeed called for the suppression of ten calendar days from the year 1582 by Pope Gregory XIII and also accounts for the fact that, ever since then, we add an extra 366th day only to century years that are also precise multiples of 400 (thereby skipping 1700, 1800, and

1900). By thus omitting three actual calendar days every four hundred years, we manage to get rid of the three superfluous days that would have accumulated over that period given that every quadrennial leap year is in fact 44 minutes and 56 seconds (the actual difference between 23 hours, 15 minutes, and 4 seconds and a full calendar day) longer than it would be if we were to measure it strictly according to nature and its periodicities.

Like the calendar year, the calendar month too is only a rough approximation of the actual natural cycle on which it is originally based. (This is true even in the Jewish, Mohammedan, and other so-called "lunar" calendars.) A precise multiple of the day, it is certainly more convenient mathematically than the actual period of twenty-nine days, twelve hours, forty-four minutes, and three seconds that elapse between any two successive new moons. In fact, only by dissociating it from the lunation have we managed to actually synchronize the month with both the day (so that every new calendar month would begin at midnight, along with a new calendar day) and the year (so that the beginning of a new calendar year would always coincide with that of a new calendar month).[25] However, from a strictly physiotemporal standpoint, the conventional thirty-, thirty-one-, twenty-eight-, or twenty-nine-day calendar month clearly distorts the actual relations between the earth and the moon.

Practically none of the points where these cycles conventionally begin has any natural significance. There is nothing in nature that regularly corresponds to midnight, Sunday, August 1, or New Year's Day. The fact that when our days, weeks, months, and years actually "begin" is utterly conventional further reminds us that none of the foundations of our standard system of reckoning the time is truly inevitable.[26]

The unmistakably conventional nature of our standard time-reckoning system is also evident from the fact that a standardized method of reckoning time has not always existed.[27] The Gregorian calendar has only relatively recently become more than just a European and American calendar.[28] Societies that now reckon the time in accordance with the seemingly natural (or divine) seven-day week have not always done so.[29]

Furthermore, the very effort to standardize the mental process of reckoning the time is quite recent. Prior to the official introduction of the International Date Line in 1884, the same day that was considered Sunday by anyone who came to Alaska from the United States was still considered Monday by those who came there from Russia.[30] (Indeed, that was precisely the kind of problem that inspired the ending of Jules Verne's novel *Around the World in Eighty Days*, written in 1873.)[31]

In fact, even standard clock time is a relatively modern phenomenon, and there is far more temporal coordination between people who are living in Denver and Nairobi today than there was between people who were living in Philadelphia and Baltimore only a little more than a century ago. Not until 1840, when railroad companies began using Greenwich time throughout Britain, was the first serious attempt made to standardize clock-time reckoning beyond the strictly local level.[32] Only as they became parts of a single transportation network (which understandably called for a single timetable) did local communities that had until then led a rather insular existence reach a point when they could no longer afford to reckon the time independently of one another.

Nor could they afford to do so once instantaneous telecommunication became a technological reality in the mid-1830s. A person who is trying to place a telephone call from Caracas to Paris or Singapore cannot possibly be oblivious to the local times there. Nor, for that matter, can a stockbroker or television reporter in London today afford not to be fully synchronized with his associates in Tokyo or New York. No such concerns, however, could have even existed prior to the invention of the telegraph only 160 years ago.

Despite its obvious ubiquity, our standard system of reckoning the time is still not absolutely universal even today. Its international status notwithstanding, the Gregorian calendar is still not even the most significant framework within which Orthodox Jews, Muslims, or Bahai's, for example, reckon the time. Nor, for that matter, is it all that clear how relevant are clock time or the week to people who are retired or unemployed.[33]

While perhaps somewhat exceptional, such cases nevertheless help us separate the merely conventional from the truly inevitable. People who do not know "the time" or have absolutely no idea what day or year "it is" may very well be considered cognitive deviants, but they certainly keep reminding us that thinking in a social manner is by no means natural.

8 /

Conclusion

The six mental processes I have examined here (perception, attention, classification, semiotic association, memory, and time reckoning) certainly do not exhaust the phenomenon we call "thinking." Nonetheless, probing their social underpinnings gives us at least a general idea of what cognitive sociology has to offer the modern science of the mind.[1]

There are numerous matters which cognitive science has thus far been unable to address. For example, it cannot explain why the "cubist" style of perceiving objects evolved only in the twentieth century, or how secretaries figure out which of the things that are said at meetings ought to be included in the minutes and which ones can be officially ignored. Nor can it account for the strong aversion of Gypsies to animals that shed their skin, or for cognitive battles over the mental delineation of "science" and "work." Addressing such matters certainly calls for a cognitive *sociology*.

By the same token, only a sociology of perception can account for the fact that we now notice "Freudian" slips that would have been ignored a hundred years ago. Only a sociology of attention would dwell on the striking contrast between the rigid style of mental focusing so prevalent among lawyers and the more "fluid" style so distinctively characteristic of detectives. And only a sociology of classification can account for the fact that, by the time she was three, my daughter could already tell that I was only kidding when I suggested that she bring her friend some lima beans as a birthday present.

More than any of the other sciences of the mind, cognitive sociology highlights the fact that what goes on inside our heads is also affected by our social environment. In probing the social dimension of our cognition, it reminds us that we think not only as individuals and as human beings, but also as members of particular communities with certain distinctive cognitive traditions that affect the way we process the world in our minds.

Like the other sciences of the mind, cognitive sociology rejects the individualistic vision of the solitary thinker whose thinking is strictly personal, thus calling attention to the fact that much of what we "remember" actually happened before we were born, and reminding us that it is not just particular individuals who happen to associate whiteness with purity and handwriting with intimacy. Focusing primarily on the impersonal "mindscapes" we share in common, it likewise highlights the fact that we reckon the time in the same terms that others do and by and large ignore the same things that they do.

Yet unlike the other sciences of the mind, cognitive sociology is careful not to mistake impersonality for universality, reminding us that, when rejecting cognitive individualism, we need not go all the way to the other extreme of fully embracing cognitive universalism. After all, though the fact that the framework within which we reckon the time is shared by others around us suggests that it is not just personal, it is by no means universal.

Focusing primarily on our cognitive commonality as human beings certainly helps cognitive scientists identify universal patterns in the way we process information, form concepts, or access our memory, yet it also helps them ignore the unmistakably nonuniversal mental *soft*ware we use when we think. It is their implicit universalistic bias, for example, that keeps cognitive psychologists from addressing the rather striking difference between the ancient and modern Greek visions of the universe or between the way morticians and theologians see death. By the same token, despite their considerable interest in the schematic nature of human cognition, only few of them have explicitly noted that "schemas" are conventional, *socio*mental structures grounded in culturally, historically, and subculturally specific cognitive traditions (of perceiving, attending, associating, and remembering) that we learn as part of our cognitive socialization.

While resisting the Romantic appeal of cognitive individualism by calling attention to the similar manner in which we use particular concepts or reckon the time, cognitive sociology also tries to resist cognitive universalism by highlighting our cognitive differences as members of different thought communities. It thus tries to show that our mindscapes are not so different as to be utterly idiosyncratic yet at the same time also not so similar as to be absolutely universal.

Highlighting what both cognitive individualism and universalism normally ignore is a tough epistemological challenge that resembles driving in a tunnel without bumping into either of its walls. Yet the ultimate goal should be to develop an integrative, multilevel approach to cognition that views us *both* as individuals, as human beings, and as social beings. Since cognitive individualism addresses only the first of those three levels and cognitive universalism basically confines itself to the second, each of them by itself is somewhat limited in its scope. In focusing specifically on the third, intermediate level, cognitive sociology helps widen that scope as well as avoid the reductive tendencies normally associated with those two extremes. Ultimately, only a science that addresses *all* three levels can provide a truly comprehensive account of how we think.

/ Notes

1. The Sociology of the Mind

1. See also Charles O. Frake, "The Ethnographic Study of Cognitive Systems," in Stephen A. Tyler (ed.), *Cognitive Anthropology* (New York: Holt, Rinehart, and Winston, 1969 [1962]), p. 36.

2. See Stephen M. Downes, "Socializing Naturalized Philosophy of Science," *Philosophy of Science* 60 (1993): 452–468.

3. On the rise of the modern science of the mind, see Howard Gardner, *The Mind's New Science: A History of the Cognitive Revolution* (New York: Basic, 1985).

4. On the tension between empiricism and rationalism within psychology, see also Edwin G. Boring, *Sensation and Perception in the History of Experimental Psychology* (New York: Appleton-Century-Crofts, 1942), pp. 28–34.

5. Sigmund Freud, *The Interpretation of Dreams* (London: Hogarth Press, 1953 [1899]).

6. The term "sociology of thinking" was first used by Ludwik Fleck in "The Problem of Epistemology," in Robert S. Cohen and Thomas Schnelle (eds.), *Cognition and Fact: Materials on Ludwik Fleck* (Dordrecht: D. Reidel, 1986 [1936]), pp. 80, 98, 105. See also Fleck, "To Look, To See, To Know," in Cohen and Schnelle, *Cognition and Fact*, pp. 150–151.

7. The term "sociomental" has been jointly developed with Mary Chayko. See Eviatar Zerubavel, "Horizons: On the Sociomental Foundations of Relevance," *Social Research* 60 (1993): 398.

8. The actual term "cognitive sociology" was first used by Aaron Cicourel as the title of a collection of essays on language and social interaction—*Cognitive Sociology: Language and Meaning in Social Interaction* (New York: Free Press, 1974). What Cicourel seemed to envision as the

actual scope of such a field, however, was quite different from what I pro-
pose here. Cognitive sociology should also not be confused with what psychologists call "social cognition," since it deals not only with the cognition
of social objects but with the social foundations of cognition in general.

9. For a somewhat similar call to integrate the perspectives of the
"social representations" and "social schema" traditions in contemporary
social psychology, see Martha Augoustinos and John M. Innes, "Towards an
Integration of Social Representations and Social Schema Theory," *British
Journal of Social Psychology* 29 (1990): 213–231. On the similar need to
integrate the work on cognition done in developmental and cognitive psychology and in cultural anthropology, see Michael Cole, "The Zone of Prox-
imal Development: Where Culture and Cognition Create Each Other," in
James V. Wertsch (ed.), *Culture, Communication, and Cognition: Vygotskian
Perspectives* (Cambridge: Cambridge University Press, 1985), pp. 146–161.

10. See also Lauren B. Resnick, "Shared Cognition: Thinking as Social
Practice," in Lauren B. Resnick, John M. Levine, and Stephanie D. Teasley
(eds.), *Perspectives on Socially Shared Cognition* (Washington, D.C.: American Psychological Association, 1991), pp. 1–20.

11. Emile Durkheim, *The Elementary Forms of Religious Life* (New
York: Free Press, 1995 [1912]), pp. 433–440; Emile Durkheim, "The Dual-
ism of Human Nature and Its Social Conditions," in Robert N. Bellah (ed.),
Emile Durkheim: On Morality and Society (Chicago: University of Chicago
Press, 1973 [1914]), pp. 149–163.

12. Karl Mannheim, *Ideology and Utopia: An Introduction to the Sociology of Knowledge* (New York: Harvest, 1936 [1929]), p. 3.

13. George H. Mead, *Mind, Self, and Society: From the Standpoint of A
Social Behaviorist* (Chicago: University of Chicago Press, 1934), pp. 42–134;
Peter L. Berger and Thomas Luckmann, *The Social Construction of Reality:
A Treatise in the Sociology of Knowledge* (Garden City, N.Y.: Doubleday
Anchor, 1967 [1966]), pp. 36–41; Alfred Schutz and Thomas Luckmann,
The Structures of the Life-World (Evanston, Ill.: Northwestern University
Press, 1973), pp. 233–235, 249–250.

14. It was Alfred Schutz who introduced the phenomenological con-
cept "intersubjectivity" to sociology. See Alfred Schutz, *The Phenomenology
of the Social World* (Evanston, Ill.: Northwestern University Press, 1967
[1932]), pp. 97–138; Alfred Schutz, *Collected Papers* (The Hague: Martinus
Nijhoff, 1973), vol. 1, pp. 10–15, 112, 150–183, 312–329. On the role of

intersubjectivity in communication, see Harold Garfinkel, "Studies of the Routine Grounds of Everyday Activities," in *Studies in Ethnomethodology* (Englewood Cliffs, N.J.: Prentice-Hall, 1967 [1964]), pp. 35–75; Ragnar Rommetveit, "Language Acquisition as Increasing Linguistic Structuring of Experience and Symbolic Behavior Control," in James V. Wertsch (ed.), *Culture, Communication, and Cognition: Vygotskian Perspectives* (Cambridge: Cambridge University Press, 1985), pp. 183–204; Barbara Rogoff, *Apprenticeship in Thinking: Cognitive Development in Social Context* (New York: Oxford University Press, 1990), pp. 71–74, 148–150; Emanuel A. Schegloff, "Repair after Next Turn: The Last Structurally Provided Defense of Intersubjectivity in Conversation," *American Journal of Sociology* 97 (1992): 1296.

15. For an early statement on such "shared cognition," see Emile Durkheim, *The Division of Labor in Society* (New York: Free Press, 1984 [1893]), pp. 38–39. See also Berger and Luckmann, *The Social Construction of Reality*, p. 23; Serge Moscovici, "The Phenomenon of Social Representations," in Robert M. Farr and Serge Moscovici (eds.), *Social Representations* (Cambridge: Cambridge University Press, 1982), pp. 3–70; Resnick, "Shared Cognition."

16. The term "thought communities" was first used by Ludwik Fleck in *Genesis and Development of a Scientific Fact* (Chicago: University of Chicago Press, 1979 [1935]), pp. 45, 103. See also pp. 38–51, 98–111 for his general discussion of "thought collectives." For a classic analysis of thought communities, see Mannheim, *Ideology and Utopia*. For somewhat similar discussions of "epistemic" and "discourse" communities, see also Burkart Holzner, *Reality Construction in Society* (Cambridge, Mass.: Schenkman, 1968), p. 69; Resnick, "Shared Cognition," p. 8.

17. See, for example, Georg Lukács, *History and Class Consciousness: Studies in Marxist Dialectics* (Cambridge, Mass.: MIT Press, 1971 [1923]), pp. 83–87; Berger and Luckmann, *The Social Construction of Reality*, pp. 89, 134–135.

18. See also Durkheim, *The Elementary Forms of Religious Life*, pp. 12–18.

19. For a classic analysis of this world, see Berger and Luckmann, *The Social Construction of Reality*.

20. For an extensive discussion of various methodological implications of such an approach, see Michael Cole and Barbara Means, *Comparative*

Studies of How People Think: An Introduction (Cambridge, Mass.: Harvard University Press, 1981).

21. See Eviatar Zerubavel, *The Fine Line: Making Distinctions in Everyday Life* (Chicago: University of Chicago Press, 1993 [1991]), pp. 52–53, 106.

22. See James F. Hamill, *Ethno-Logic: The Anthropology of Human Reasoning* (Urbana: University of Illinois Press, 1990), pp. 73–101.

23. See, for example, Gustav Jahoda, *Crossroads between Culture and Mind: Continuities and Change in Theories of Human Nature* (Cambridge, Mass.: Harvard University Press, 1993), pp. 75–78, 140–153, 170–188. For an explicit articulation of the distinctive intellectual thrust of this tradition, see, for example, Benjamin L. Whorf, *Language, Thought, and Reality* (Cambridge, Mass.: MIT Press, 1956).

24. On the merits of a comparative, cross-cultural cognitive psychology, see, for example, J. W. Berry and P. R. Dasen, "Introduction: History and Method in the Cross-Cultural Study of Cognition," in J. W. Berry and P. R. Dasen (eds.), *Culture and Cognition: Readings in Cross-Cultural Psychology* (London: Methuen, 1974), pp. 12–20.

25. Our tendency to reify the social world is itself at least partly a function of its historicity. Not having been around at the time when something was introduced, we often assume that it has *always* been there. Hence our tendency to take for granted everything that was already in the world when we first entered it. Americans who are born today are thus much more likely to take the presence of women and ethnic minorities on the United States Supreme Court for granted than their grandparents, for the same reason that they would find it difficult to even imagine a world with no television, computers, or cars.

26. See, for example, Mannheim, *Ideology and Utopia;* Fleck, *Genesis and Development of a Scientific Fact,* pp. 103–107; Tamotsu Shibutani, "Reference Groups as Perspectives," *American Journal of Sociology* 60 (1955): 562–569; Sherry Turkle, *The Second Self: Computers and the Human Spirit* (New York: Touchstone, 1985 [1984]), pp. 318–319.

27. See also Fleck, *Genesis and Development of a Scientific Fact,* p. 99 on cognitive "heretics."

28. See also Deborah L. Pool, Richard A. Shweder, and Nancy C. Much, "Culture as a Cognitive System: Differentiated Role Understandings in Children and Other Savages," in E. Tory Higgins, Diane N. Ruble, and

Willard W. Hartup (eds.), *Social Cognition and Social Development: A Sociocultural Perspective* (Cambridge: Cambridge University Press, 1983), p. 195 on "norms for thinking."

29. Durkheim, *The Elementary Forms of Religious Life*, pp. 16–17; Fleck, *Genesis and Development of a Scientific Fact*, pp. 100–101. See also Emile Durkheim, *The Rules of Sociological Method* (New York: Free Press, 1982 [1895]), pp. 51–53.

30. Zerubavel, *The Fine Line*, pp. 16–17, 62–64; Eviatar Zerubavel, "Lumping and Splitting: Notes on Social Classification," *Sociological Forum* 11 (1996): 421–433; Kristen Purcell, "In a League of Their Own: Mental Leveling and the Creation of Social Comparability in Sport" *Sociological Forum* 11 (1996): 435–456.

31. See, for example, Cindy D. Clark, *Flights of Fancy, Leaps of Faith: Children's Myths in Contemporary America* (Chicago: University of Chicago Press, 1995), pp. 5–21, 37–58. See also Zerubavel, *The Fine Line*, pp. 81–83.

32. As a four-year-old, I was likewise more interested in counting the seats in a stadium than in following the athletic action taking place in it.

33. See also, in this regard, Jean Piaget, *The Moral Judgment of the Child* (New York: Free Press, 1965 [1932]), pp. 40–41; Rommetveit, "Language Acquisition," pp. 190–191.

34. I am using the term "sociocognitive" in the sense it has been used by Rommetveit, "Language Acquisition," and Resnick, "Shared Cognition," pp. 3–4, 15–16, rather than in the narrower sense used by social and developmental psychologists who are interested only in the cognition of social objects.

35. On how we learn later on as adults to rediscover those spaces, see Christopher Alexander et al., *A Pattern Language: Towns, Buildings, Construction* (New York: Oxford University Press, 1977), pp. 518–522. See also Betty Edwards, *Drawing on the Right Side of the Brain: A Course in Enhancing Creativity and Artistic Confidence* (Los Angeles: J. P. Tarcher, 1979), pp. 98–113; Betty Edwards, *Drawing on the Artist Within: A Guide to Innovation, Invention, Imagination, and Creativity* (New York: Simon and Schuster, 1986), pp. 155–165; Wayne Brekhus, "Studying the Unmarked: Redirecting Sociology's Focus" (unpublished manuscript, Rutgers University, Department of Sociology, 1996).

36. See, for example, Lev S. Vygotsky, *Mind in Society: The Development of Higher Psychological Processes* (Cambridge, Mass.: Harvard University Press, 1978).

37. In fact, towards the end of his life, even Piaget himself came to recognize the importance of cultural influences on cognitive development. See Jean Piaget, "Need and Significance of Cross-Cultural Studies in Genetic Psychology," *International Journal of Psychology* 1 (1966): 3–13. See also P. R. Dasen, "Cross-Cultural Piagetian Research: A Summary," *Journal of Cross-Cultural Psychology* 3 (1972): 23–39; William Damon, "Why Study Social-Cognitive Development?" *Human Development* 22 (1979): 206–211; Mary Gauvain, "Sociocultural Processes in the Development of Thinking," in Jeanette Altarriba (ed.), *Cognition and Culture: A Cross-Cultural Approach to Cognitive Psychology* (Amsterdam: North-Holland, 1993), pp. 299–316.

38. Vygotsky, *Mind in Society,* pp. 56–57, 90; Rogoff, *Apprenticeship in Thinking.* On the idea of cognitive apprenticeship, see also Fleck, *Genesis and Development of a Scientific Fact,* p. 104. See also Nira Granott, "Unit of Analysis in Transit: From the Individual's Knowledge to the Ensemble Process," *Mind, Culture, and Activity* (in press).

39. See, for example, Alexander R. Luria, *Cognitive Development: Its Cultural and Social Foundations* (Cambridge, Mass.: Harvard University Press, 1976 [1974]); Walter J. Ong, *Orality and Literacy: The Technologizing of the Word* (London: Methuen, 1982).

40. See also Rogoff, *Apprenticeship in Thinking,* p. 207.

41. See also Eviatar Zerubavel, *Hidden Rhythms: Schedules and Calendars in Social Life* (Berkeley: University of California Press, 1985 [1981]), pp. 117–124.

42. Schutz and Luckmann, *The Structures of the Life-World,* pp. 77, 229–241; Berger and Luckmann, *The Social Construction of Reality,* pp. 30–34, 54–58; Zerubavel, *The Fine Line,* p. 17.

43. Fleck, *Genesis and Development of a Scientific Fact,* pp. 45, 110.

44. Rommetveit, "Language Acquisition," pp. 186–187.

45. See, for example, Joshua Meyrowitz, *No Sense of Place: The Impact of Electronic Media on Social Behavior* (New York: Oxford University Press, 1985), pp. 79, 87, 309–310.

46. On cognitive pluralism, see also Sherry Turkle and Seymour Papert, "Epistemological Pluralism: Styles and Voices within the Computer Culture," *Signs* 16 (1990): 128–157.

47. See, for example, Lewis A. Coser, *Greedy Institutions: Patterns of Undivided Commitment* (New York: Free Press, 1974).

48. Georg Simmel, "The Web of Group Affiliations," in *Conflict and the Web of Group Affiliations* (New York: Free Press, 1964 [1908]), pp. 127–195.

49. On the cognitive implications of social mobility, see also Georg Simmel, "The Stranger," in Kurt H. Wolff (ed.), *The Sociology of Georg Simmel* (New York: Free Press, 1950 [1908]), pp. 402–408; Pitirim A. Sorokin, *Social and Cultural Mobility* (New York: Free Press, 1964 [1927]), pp. 509–515.

50. See Herbert Spencer, *The Evolution of Society* (Chicago: University of Chicago Press, 1967 [1876]), pp. 14–27.

51. On the "cognitive division of labor," see also Roy D'Andrade, *The Development of Cognitive Anthropology* (Cambridge: Cambridge University Press, 1995), p. 208. On the "division of cognitive labor" within social groups, see also Edwin Hutchins, "The Social Organization of Distributed Cognition," in Lauren B. Resnick, John M. Levine, and Stephanie D. Teasley (eds.), *Perspectives on Socially Shared Cognition* (Washington, D.C.: American Psychological Association, 1991), p. 284.

52. See also Schutz and Luckmann, *The Structures of the Life-World,* pp. 299–318; Holzner, *Reality Construction in Society,* pp. 122–142; Raymond S. Nickerson, "On the Distribution of Cognition: Some Reflections," in Gavriel Salomon (ed.), *Distributed Cognitions: Psychological and Educational Considerations* (Cambridge: Cambridge University Press, 1993), p. 241.

53. On the general distinction between primary and secondary socialization (a distinction that exists even at the level of secondary socialization itself, as evident from the difference between the "core" courses that every psychology major is required to take and the more specialized "electives" that are taken only by choice), see Berger and Luckmann, *The Social Construction of Reality,* pp. 129–147.

54. See also Mannheim, *Ideology and Utopia,* pp. 33–34.

55. See also Emile Durkheim, *Suicide: A Study in Sociology* (New York: Free Press, 1966 [1897]), pp. 157–170. As for the possible danger of *cognitive anomie,* whereby "mental Robinson Crusoes" (in a manner eerily evocative of psychotic and seriously brain-damaged individuals) might cognitively inhabit utterly personal worlds, see also Durkheim, *The Division of Labor in Society,* pp. 294–301.

56. See also, for example, Basil B. Bernstein, *Class, Codes, and Control*

(London: Routledge & Kegan Paul, 1971); Luria, *Cognitive Development,* pp. 102–133; and Sylvia Scribner, "Modes of Thinking and Ways of Speaking: Culture and Logic Reconsidered," in P. N. Johnson-Laird and P. C. Wason (eds.), *Thinking: Readings in Cognitive Science* (Cambridge: Cambridge University Press, 1977), pp. 483–500, on the social foundations of logical reasoning.

2. Social Optics

1. For some earlier attempts to do so, see Arthur Child, "The Sociology of Perception," *Journal of Genetic Psychology* 77 (1950): 293–303; Mary Douglas (ed.), *Essays in the Sociology of Perception* (London: Routledge & Kegan Paul, 1982). See also Donald M. Lowe, *History of Bourgeois Perception* (Chicago: University of Chicago Press, 1982).

2. See, for example, Solomon E. Asch, "Studies of Independence and Conformity: A Minority of One against a Unanimous Majority," *Psychological Monographs* 70, no. 9 (whole no. 416) (1956).

3. Roger W. Brown and Eric H. Lenneberg, "A Study in Language and Cognition," *Journal of Abnormal and Social Psychology* 49 (1954): 454–462. See also Luria, *Cognitive Development,* pp. 20–30.

4. See, for example, Marshall H. Segall, Donald T. Campbell, and Melville J. Herskovits, *The Influence of Culture on Visual Perception* (Indianapolis: Bobbs-Merrill, 1966), pp. 55–67, 99–171; Jan B. Deregowski, "Difficulties in Pictorial Depth Perception in Africa," *British Journal of Psychology* 59 (1968): 195–204; Luria, *Cognitive Development,* pp. 33–34, 39–45; Michael Cole and Sylvia Scribner, *Culture and Thought: A Psychological Introduction* (New York: John Wiley, 1974), pp. 67–71, 74–80; John W. Berry et al., *Cross-Cultural Psychology: Research and Applications* (Cambridge: Cambridge University Press, 1992), pp. 151–153.

5. On mental "filtration," see also Murray S. Davis, *Smut: Erotic Reality/ Obscene Ideology* (Chicago: University of Chicago Press, 1983), pp. 216–225.

6. Consider, in this regard, the "blindfold tests" done by *Down Beat* magazine, where jazz musicians are asked to comment on pieces they hear without being told the identity of the performer. See also Steven M. Cahn and L. Michael Griffel, "The Strange Case of John Shmarb: An Aesthetic Puzzle," *Journal of Aesthetics and Art Criticism* 34 (1975): 21–22.

7. See, for example, Zerubavel, *Hidden Rhythms*, pp. 23–24.

8. See, for example, Richard C. Anderson et al., "Frameworks for Comprehending Discourse," *American Educational Research Journal* 14 (1977): 367–381; Roger C. Schank and Robert P. Abelson, "Scripts, Plans, and Knowledge," in P. N. Johnson-Laird and P. C. Wason (eds.), *Thinking: Readings in Cognitive Science* (Cambridge: Cambridge University Press, 1977), pp. 421–432; David E. Rumelhart, "Schemata and the Cognitive System," in Robert S. Wyer and Thomas K. Srull (eds.), *Handbook of Social Cognition*, vol. 1 (Hillsdale, N.J.: Lawrence Erlbaum, 1984), pp. 174–176; Susan T. Fiske and Shelley E. Taylor, *Social Cognition* (New York: Addison-Wesley, 1984), pp. 151–152. See also Schutz and Luckmann, *The Structures of the Life-World*, pp. 229–241; Berger and Luckmann, *The Social Construction of Reality*, pp. 30–34, 54–58.

9. See, for example, David E. Rumelhart and Andrew Ortony, "The Representation of Knowledge in Memory," in Richard C. Anderson, Rand J. Spiro, and William E. Montague (eds.), *Schooling and the Acquisition of Knowledge* (Hillsdale, N.J.: Lawrence Erlbaum, 1977), p. 112; Fiske and Taylor, *Social Cognition*, p. 141. See also Garfinkel, "Studies of the Routine Grounds of Everyday Activities," pp. 42–65; Zerubavel, *Hidden Rhythms*, pp. 26–30.

10. Eviatar Zerubavel, *Terra Cognita: The Mental Discovery of America* (New Brunswick, N.J.: Rutgers University Press, 1992), pp. 88–96.

11. Fleck, *Genesis and Development of a Scientific Fact*.

12. Ibid.; Thomas S. Kuhn, *The Structure of Scientific Revolutions* (Chicago: University of Chicago Press, 1962), pp. 111–135. See also Eviatar Zerubavel, "If Simmel Were a Fieldworker: On Formal Sociological Theory and Analytical Field Research," *Symbolic Interaction* 3, no. 2 (1980), pp. 29–30.

13. See Zerubavel, *Terra Cognita*, pp. 96–104 and Plates 1, 2, 12, 13, 14, 19, 20, 21, 27, 28, and 29.

14. Martin Waldseemüller, *Cosmographiae Introductio* (Ann Arbor, Mich.: University Microfilms, 1966 [1507]), pp. 68–70; Zerubavel, *Terra Cognita*, pp. 80–82 and Plates 5 and 6. On Waldseemüller's tremendous cosmographic impact on sixteenth-century Europe, see Zerubavel, *Terra Cognita*, pp. 82–83 and Plates 11 and 23.

15. See Zerubavel, *Terra Cognita*, pp. 51–52.

16. On the long history of that critical yet largely overlooked discovery, see ibid., pp. 57–66.

17. Thomas Laqueur, *Making Sex: Body and Gender from the Greeks to Freud* (Cambridge, Mass.: Harvard University Press, 1990).

18. Ibid. See also Zerubavel, *The Fine Line,* pp. 46–47.

19. Fleck, *Genesis and Development of a Scientific Fact.*

20. See also Berger and Luckmann, *The Social Construction of Reality,* pp. 92–116; Davis, *Smut,* pp. 165–246.

21. See also Mannheim, *Ideology and Utopia,* pp. 78–79, 85–86, 282–283; Karsten Hundeide, "The Tacit Background of Children's Judgments," in James V. Wertsch (ed.), *Culture, Communication, and Cognition: Vygotskian Perspectives* (Cambridge: Cambridge University Press, 1985), p. 313; Donna J. Haraway, "Situated Knowledges: The Science Question in Feminism and the Privilege of Partial Perspective," in *Simians, Cyborgs, and Women: The Reinvention of Nature* (New York: Routledge, 1991), pp. 183–201.

22. On the latter, see Georg Simmel, "The Field of Sociology," in Kurt H. Wolff (ed.), *The Sociology of Georg Simmel* (New York: Free Press, 1950 [1917]), pp. 7–8.

23. Hundeide, "The Tacit Background of Children's Judgments," p. 312.

24. See, for example, ibid. On the social underpinnings of our frameworks of interpretation, see also Moscovici, "The Phenomenon of Social Representations"; Jeanette Altarriba and Wendy J. Forsythe, "The Role of Cultural Schemata in Reading Comprehension," in Jeanette Altarriba (ed.), *Cognition and Culture: A Cross-Cultural Approach to Cognitive Psychology* (Amsterdam: North-Holland, 1993), pp. 145–155.

25. On the social organization of our cognitive predispositions, see also Hutchins, "The Social Organization of Distributed Cognition," p. 295.

26. That may also explain why Frederic Bartlett's own schema theory of 1932, one of the cornerstones of psychology over the past twenty years, had virtually no influence on the field during the preceding four decades, when it was mainly dominated by empiricism! See William F. Brewer and Glenn V. Nakamura, "The Nature and Functions of Schemas," in Robert S. Wyer and Thomas K. Srull (eds.), *Handbook of Social Cognition,* vol. 1 (Hillsdale, N.J.: Lawrence Erlbaum, 1984), pp. 126–131.

27. Fleck, *Genesis and Development of a Scientific Fact,* pp. 41, 99–102,

121–123. On externality and constraint as major aspects of social phenomena in general, see Durkheim, *The Rules of Sociological Method*, pp. 50–59.

28. See also Mead, *Mind, Self, and Society*, pp. 151–163.

29. See, for example, C. Wright Mills, *The Sociological Imagination* (New York: Oxford University Press, 1967 [1959]), pp. 5–7. For a classic "optical" characterization of sociology, see also Georg Simmel, "The Problem of Sociology," in Kurt H. Wolff (ed.), *Georg Simmel, 1858–1918* (Columbus, Ohio: Ohio State University Press, 1959 [1908]), pp. 310–336; Simmel, "The Field of Sociology," pp. 7–15.

30. See also Ludwik Fleck, "Scientific Observation and Perception in General," in Robert S. Cohen and Thomas Schnelle (eds.), *Cognition and Fact: Materials on Ludwik Fleck* (Dordrecht: D. Reidel, 1986 [1935]), pp. 59–78; Fleck, "To Look, To See, To Know."

31. See also Mannheim, *Ideology and Utopia*, pp. 56–59.

32. See also Fleck, *Genesis and Development of a Scientific Fact* on "thought styles."

33. On the fundamental difference between truly collective and merely aggregate mental "visions," see Charles H. Cooley, *Social Organization: A Study of the Larger Mind* (New York: Schocken, 1962 [1909]), pp. 121–127; Durkheim, *The Elementary Forms of Religious Life*, pp. 436–437. For a more general statement, see also Durkheim, *Suicide*, pp. 297–325.

34. See, for example, Child, "The Sociology of Perception," pp. 295–300.

35. See, for example, Ralph E. Reynolds et al., "Cultural Schemata and Reading Comprehension," *Reading Research Quarterly* 17 (1982): 353–366.

36. See, for example, Davis, *Smut*, pp. 26–30.

3. The Social Gates of Consciousness

1. See, for example, James J. Gibson, *The Perception of the Visual World* (Boston: Houghton Mifflin, 1950), pp. 27–29.

2. Edgar Rubin, *Visuell wahrgenommene Figuren* (Copenhagen: Gyldendal, 1921 [1915]).

3. See, for example, Anton Ehrenzweig, *The Psychoanalysis of Artistic Vision and Hearing: An Introduction to a Theory of Unconscious Perception* (London: Sheldon, 1975 [1953]); Kenneth L. Pike, *Language in Relation to a Unified Theory of the Structure of Human Behavior* (The Hague: Mouton,

1967 [1954]), pp. 78–80, 98–119; Erving Goffman, *Behavior in Public Places: Notes on the Social Organization of Gatherings* (New York: Free Press, 1963), pp. 24, 33–148; Garfinkel, "Studies of the Routine Grounds of Everyday Activities"; Zerubavel, *Hidden Rhythms*, pp. 19–30; Zerubavel, *The Fine Line*, pp. 6, 87, 93, 98, 119, 121; Zerubavel, "Horizons."

4. For a more general statement, see also Gregory Bateson, "A Theory of Play and Fantasy," in *Steps to an Ecology of Mind* (New York: Ballantine, 1972 [1955]), p. 187.

5. Wolfgang Köhler, *Gestalt Psychology: An Introduction to New Concepts in Modern Psychology* (New York: New American Library, 1947), pp. 84, 93; Zerubavel, *The Fine Line*, pp. 1, 6, 118–119.

6. See, for example, Herman A. Witkin, "Psychological Differentiation and Forms of Pathology," *Journal of Abnormal Psychology* 70 (1965): 319; Thomas Freeman, John L. Cameron, and Andrew McGhie, *Studies on Psychosis: Descriptive, Psycho-analytic, and Psychological Aspects* (New York: International Universities Press, 1966), pp. 72–87, 160–161, 190–191; Zerubavel, *The Fine Line*, p. 84.

7. See also Goffman, *Behavior in Public Places*, pp. 50–53.

8. Zerubavel, *The Fine Line*, pp. 2, 16. See also Anthony F. Wallace and John Atkins, "The Meaning of Kinship Terms," *American Anthropologist* 62 (1960): 67.

9. See, for example, Bateson, "A Theory of Play and Fantasy"; Erving Goffman, *Frame Analysis: An Essay on the Organization of Experience* (New York: Harper Colophon, 1974); Zerubavel, *The Fine Line*, pp. 10–13. See also Georg Simmel, "Sociability: An Example of Pure, or Formal Sociology," in Kurt H. Wolff (ed.), *The Sociology of Georg Simmel* (New York: Free Press, 1950 [1917]), pp. 45–53.

10. Goffman, *Frame Analysis*, pp. 201–246.

11. Alfred Schutz, "On Multiple Realities," in *Collected Papers, vol.1: The Problem of Social Reality* (The Hague: Martinus Nijhoff, 1973 [1945]), p. 233; Goffman, *Frame Analysis*, pp. 251–269; Zerubavel, *The Fine Line*, pp. 11, 94–95.

12. See also Erving Goffman, "Fun in Games," in *Encounters: Two Studies in the Sociology of Interaction* (Indianapolis: Bobbs-Merrill, 1961), pp. 19–34; Purcell, "In a League of Their Own".

13. See also Goffman, "Fun in Games," pp. 63–64.

14. Erving Goffman, *The Presentation of Self in Everyday Life* (Garden

City, N.Y.: Doubleday Anchor, 1959), pp. 151–153. See also Erving Goffman, "Footing," in *Forms of Talk* (Philadelphia: University of Pennsylvania Press, 1981 [1979]), pp. 131–137.

15. See, for example, John Hotchkiss, "Children and Conduct in a Ladino Community in Chiapas, Mexico," *American Anthropologist* 69 (1967): 711–718; Rogoff, *Apprenticeship in Thinking*, pp. 124–126.

16. Peter Singer, *The Expanding Circle: Ethics and Sociobiology* (New York: Farrar, Straus & Giroux, 1981).

17. See, for example, Kurt Koffka, *Principles of Gestalt Psychology* (New York: Harcourt, Brace & World, 1935), pp. 106–210. See also Herman A. Witkin et al., *Psychological Differentiation: Studies of Development* (Potomac, Md.: Lawrence Erlbaum Associates, 1974 [1962]).

18. See, for example, Howard Goldiner, "Getting Out of the Box: Brain Teasers and the Constraints of Common Sense" (paper presented at the Stone Symposium of the Society of Symbolic Interaction, February 1992), pp. 18–20.

19. Dale Spender, *Man Made Language* (London: Routledge & Kegan Paul, 1980), p. 165. See also Janice Haaken, "Field Dependence Research: A Historical Analysis of a Psychological Construct," *Signs* 13 (1988): 312; Zerubavel, *The Fine Line*, p. 116.

20. See, for example, Edward T. Hall, *The Hidden Dimension* (Garden City, N.Y.: Doubleday, 1966), p. 140.

21. See, for example, John W. Berry, "Ecological and Cultural Factors in Spatial Perceptual Development," *Canadian Journal of Behavioural Science* 3 (1971): 324–336.

22. Felipe Fernández-Armesto (ed.), *The Times Atlas of World Exploration: 3,000 Years of Exploring, Explorers, and Mapmaking* (New York: HarperCollins, 1991), pp. 26–27.

23. See Zerubavel, *The Fine Line*, p. 105.

24. For some examples of "environmental" art, see Luigi Pirandello, *Tonight We Improvise* (New York: Samuel French, 1960 [1932]); Allan Kaprow, *Assemblage, Environments, and Happenings* (New York: Harry N. Abrams, 1966); Richard Schechner, *Environmental Theater* (New York: Hawthorn, 1973). See also Zerubavel, *The Fine Line*, pp. 108–112.

25. See, for example, Johanna Foster, "Condom Negotiation and the Politics of Relevance" (unpublished manuscript, Rutgers University, Department of Sociology, 1995).

26. Christopher Stone, *Should Trees Have Standing?: Toward Legal Rights for Natural Objects* (Los Altos, Calif.: William Kaufmann, 1974), pp. 6–7.

27. Peter Singer, *Animal Liberation: A New Ethic for Our Treatment of Animals* (New York: Discus, 1977), p. 1. Indeed, even two centuries later, one can still come across a mainstream political cartoon in which animals sarcastically complain that "President-Elect Clinton's cabinet appointments do not reflect America's diversity . . . They're all humans!" (*Newsweek*, January 4, 1993, p. 13).

28. Sigmund Freud, *The Psychopathology of Everyday Life* (New York: W. W. Norton, 1960 [1901]).

29. Simon Mitton (ed.), *The Cambridge Encyclopaedia of Astronomy* (New York: Crown, 1977), p. 237.

30. Kuhn, *The Structure of Scientific Revolutions*, p. 116.

31. Hall, *The Hidden Dimension*.

32. Kuhn, *The Structure of Scientific Revolutions*, pp. 111, 122.

33. From a publicity blurb by T. C. Schelling for Goffman's *Strategic Interaction*. It appears on the back cover of the 1970 paperback edition of Ray Birdwhistell's *Kinesics and Context*, published by the University of Pennsylvania Press.

34. See also Hundeide, "The Tacit Background of Children's Judgments," p. 314.

35. See also Purcell, "In a League of Their Own."

36. See, for example, Myron Rothbart, Mark Evans, and Solomon Fulero, "Recall for Confirming Events: Memory Processes and the Maintenance of Social Stereotypes," *Journal of Experimental Social Psychology* 15 (1979): 343–355; Galen V. Bodenhausen, "Stereotypic Biases in Social Decision Making and Memory: Testing Process Models of Stereotype Use," *Journal of Personality and Social Psychology* 55 (1988): 726–737.

37. Frederic C. Bartlett, *Remembering: A Study in Experimental and Social Psychology* (Cambridge: Cambridge University Press, 1932), pp. 254–255.

38. Simmel, "The Field of Sociology," pp. 7–8; Rudolf Heberle, "The Sociology of Georg Simmel: The Forms of Social Interaction," in Harry E. Barnes, *An Introduction to the History of Sociology* (Chicago: University of Chicago Press, 1948), pp. 251–252. See also Eviatar Zerubavel, *Patterns of*

Time in Hospital Life: A Sociological Perspective (Chicago: University of Chicago Press, 1979), pp. xvi–xviii.

39. See also Christena Nippert-Eng, "It's About Time," *Qualitative Sociology* 18 (1995): 503–505.

40. Kuhn, *The Structure of Scientific Revolutions.*

41. See also Goffman, *The Presentation of Self in Everyday Life,* pp. 229–233; Goffman, *Behavior in Public Places,* pp. 83–88.

42. Goffman, "Fun in Games," pp. 19–26.

43. On the latter, see Purcell, "In a League of Their Own."

44. Arlie Hochschild, *The Managed Heart: Commercialization of Human Feeling* (Berkeley: University of California Press, 1983).

45. See also Christena E. Nippert-Eng, *Home and Work: Negotiating Boundaries through Everyday Life* (Chicago: University of Chicago Press, 1996), p. 12.

46. See, for example, Herbert J. Gans, *Deciding What's News: A Study of CBS Evening News, NBC Nightly News, Newsweek, and Time* (New York: Random House, 1979).

47. Eviatar Zerubavel, "The Rigid, the Fuzzy, and the Flexible: Notes on the Mental Sculpting of Academic Identity," *Social Research* 62 (1995): 1097.

48. Such mental censorship exemplifies the sad consequences of the social pressure not to venture beyond the horizons of the inevitably parochial mental ghettos created by one's various thought communities. To appreciate the tremendous price we usually pay for such institutionalized narrow-mindedness, note that the ability to integrate conventionally separate mental fields is in fact one of the key elements of creativity. See Arthur Koestler, *The Act of Creation* (New York: Macmillan, 1964); Mattei Dogan and Robert Pahre, *Creative Marginality: Innovation at the Intersections of the Social Sciences* (Boulder: Westview, 1990); Zerubavel, *The Fine Line,* p. 117. See also Jonathan Miller, *The Body in Question* (New York: Random House, 1978).

49. On erotic focusing, see also Davis, *Smut,* pp. 27–30, 40–41.

50. On the sociomental foundations of perversity, see ibid., pp. 133–139, 144–150, 156–159; Zerubavel, *The Fine Line,* pp. 40–41, 44; Wayne Brekhus, "Social Marking and the Mental Coloring of Identity: Sexual Identity Construction and Maintenance in the United States," *Sociological Forum* 11 (1996): 497–522.

4. The Social Division of the World

1. See Nippert-Eng, *Home and Work*.

2. Zerubavel, *The Fine Line*, pp. 5–32.

3. On the sociomental foundations of such "proximity," see also Edmund Leach, "Anthropological Aspects of Language: Animal Categories and Verbal Abuse," in Eric H. Lenneberg (ed.), *New Directions in the Study of Language* (Cambridge, Mass.: MIT Press, 1964), pp. 36–37, 43–44; Marshall Sahlins, *Culture and Practical Reason* (Chicago: University of Chicago Press, 1976), pp. 173–175.

4. See also Marvin Harris, "Referential Ambiguity in the Calculus of Brazilian Racial Identity," *Southwestern Journal of Anthropology* 26 (1970): 1–14; F. James Davis, *Who Is Black?: One Nation's Definition* (University Park, Penn.: Pennsylvania State University Press, 1991), pp. 99–105, 119–122.

5. See also Charles O. Frake, "The Diagnosis of Disease among the Subanun of Mindanao," *American Anthropologist* 63 (1961): 113–132.

6. See, for example, Kurt Lewin, "Some Social-Psychological Differences between the United States and Germany," in *Resolving Social Conflicts: Selected Papers on Group Dynamics* (London: Souvenir, 1973 [1936]), pp. 18–25; Hall, *The Hidden Dimension*, pp. 131–164.

7. See, for example, Viviana A. Zelizer, "Payments and Social Ties," *Sociological Forum* 11 (1996): 481–495. See also Viviana A. Zelizer, *The Social Meaning of Money: Pin Money, Paychecks, Poor Relief, and Other Currencies* (New York: Basic Books, 1994).

8. On the classic case of color categories, see, for example, John R. Taylor, *Linguistic Categorization: Prototypes in Linguistic Theory* (Oxford: Oxford University Press, 1995), 2nd ed., pp. 3–5.

9. Gary Witherspoon, *Language and Art in the Navajo Universe* (Ann Arbor: University of Michigan Press, 1977), p. 121.

10. See, for example, Benjamin L. Whorf, "Science and Linguistics," in *Language, Thought, and Reality*, pp. 207–215; Benjamin L. Whorf, "Language, Mind, and Reality," in *Language, Thought, and Reality*, pp. 258–263; John B. Carroll and Joseph B. Casagrande, "The Functions of Language Classifications in Behavior," in Eleanor E. Maccoby, Theodore M. Newcomb, and Eugene L. Hartley (eds.), *Readings in Social Psychology* (New York: Holt, Rinehart and Winston, 1958), 3rd ed., pp. 18–31.

11. Zerubavel, *The Fine Line*, pp. 21–22.

12. See, for example, Lucien Lévy-Bruhl, *How Natives Think* (New York: Washington Square Press, 1966 [1910]).

13. Hence the value of works such as Claude Lévi-Strauss's *The Savage Mind* (Chicago: University of Chicago Press, 1966 [1962]).

14. See, for example, Mary Douglas, *Natural Symbols: Explorations in Cosmology* (New York: Vintage, 1973 [1970]); Mary Douglas, "Self Evidence," in *Implicit Meanings: Essays in Anthropology* (London: Routledge & Kegan Paul, 1978 [1975]), pp. 276–318; Michèle Lamont, *Money, Morals, and Markets: The Culture of the French and the American Upper-Middle Class* (Chicago: University of Chicago Press, 1992).

15. On "the rigid mind," see Zerubavel, *The Fine Line*, pp. 33–60. See also Mary Douglas, *Purity and Danger: An Analysis of Concepts of Pollution and Taboo* (New York: Frederick A. Praeger, 1966).

16. Mary Douglas, "Deciphering a Meal," in *Implicit Meanings: Essays in Anthropology* (London: Routledge & Kegan Paul, 1978 [1972]), pp. 263–273; Douglas, "Self Evidence," pp. 303–307; Zerubavel, *Hidden Rhythms*, pp. 110–137; Zerubavel, *The Fine Line*, pp. 53–55.

17. Anne Sutherland, *Gypsies: The Hidden Americans* (London: Tavistock, 1975), pp. 13, 149–150, 247–248, 258–259, 264–271; Judith Okely, *The Traveller-Gypsies* (Cambridge: Cambridge University Press, 1983), pp. 80–85, 91–95, 101–103, 154–156; Zerubavel, *The Fine Line*, pp. 52–53.

18. On "the fuzzy mind," see Zerubavel, *The Fine Line*, pp. 81–114.

19. On "the flexible mind," see ibid., pp. 120–122; Zerubavel, "The Rigid, the Fuzzy, and the Flexible," pp. 1099–1102.

20. David F. Aberle, "Some Sources of Flexibility in Navaho Social Organization," *Southwestern Journal of Anthropology* 19 (1963): 1–8; W. W. Hill, "The Status of the Hermaphrodite and the Transvestite in Navaho Culture," *American Anthropologist* 37 (1935): 274–276; Donald N. Michael, "A Cross-Cultural Investigation of Closure," *Journal of Abnormal and Social Psychology* 48 (1953): 225–226.

21. Edmund S. Carpenter, *Eskimo* (Toronto: University of Toronto Press, 1959); W. E. Willmott, "The Flexibility of Eskimo Social Organization," in Victor F. Valentine and Frank G. Vallee (eds.), *Eskimo of the Canadian Arctic* (Toronto: McClelland and Stewart, 1968 [1960]), pp. 151, 155; Heluiz C. Washburne, *Land of the Good Shadows* (New York: John Day, 1940).

22. Zerubavel, *The Fine Line*, pp. 57–60, 87–103.

23. Douglas, *Purity and Danger*.

24. Durkheim, *The Elementary Forms of Religious Life*, pp. 34–38.

25. On the "negative cult" designed to keep the sacred and the profane apart from one another, see ibid., pp. 303–329. See also Zerubavel, *Hidden Rhythms*, pp. 101–105, 110–126.

26. Zerubavel, *Hidden Rhythms*, pp. 147–166.

27. See, for example, Miwako Kidahashi, "Dual Organization: A Study of a Japanese-Owned Firm in the United States" (Ph.D. diss., Columbia University, Department of Sociology, 1987), pp. 255–278.

28. For the numerous manifestations of the rigid mind in bureaucracy, see also Max Weber, *Economy and Society: An Outline of Interpretive Sociology* (Berkeley: University of California Press, 1978 [1925]), pp. 219, 957; Nippert-Eng, *Home and Work*.

29. Zerubavel, *The Fine Line*, pp. 96–103.

30. See Ehrenzweig, *The Psychoanalysis of Artistic Vision and Hearing*.

31. See Murray S. Davis, *Intimate Relations* (New York: Free Press, 1973), pp. 169–205; Zerubavel, *The Fine Line*, pp. 87–89.

32. See Zerubavel, *The Fine Line*, pp. 38–41, 44–45.

33. Ibid., pp. 90–96.

34. See, for example, Ian Hamnett, "Ambiguity, Classification and Change: The Function of Riddles," *Man* 2 (1967): 379–392; Ragnar Johnson, "Two Realms and a Joke: Bisociation Theories of Joking," *Semiotica* 16 (1976): 195–221; Zerubavel, *The Fine Line*, pp. 93–96; Murray S. Davis, *What's So Funny? The Comic Conception of Culture and Society* (Chicago: University of Chicago Press, 1993), pp. 18–20.

35. See Paul Bouissac, "Circus Performance as Ritual: An Aspect of Animal Acts," in *Circus and Culture: A Semiotic Approach* (Bloomington: Indiana University Press, 1976), pp. 108–122.

36. See Mikhail Bakhtin, *Rabelais and His World* (Cambridge, Mass.: MIT Press, 1968 [1965]), pp. 10, 40, 90, 264, 411; Peter Stallybrass and Allon White, *The Politics and Poetics of Transgression* (Ithaca, N.Y.: Cornell University Press, 1986).

37. Davis, *What's So Funny?*

38. Zerubavel, *The Fine Line*, pp. 92–93.

39. On masks, see A. David Napier, *Masks, Transformation, and Paradox* (Berkeley: University of California Press, 1986), pp. 1–29.

40. See Paul DiMaggio, "Cultural Entrepreneurship in Nineteenth-Century Boston, Part II: The Classification and Framing of American Art," *Media, Culture and Society* 4 (1982): 303–322.

41. See, for example, Joel Williamson, *New People: Miscegenation and Mulattoes in the United States* (New York: Free Press, 1980); Virginia R. Domínguez, *White by Definition: Social Classification in Creole Louisiana* (New Brunswick, N.J.: Rutgers University Press, 1986); Davis, *Who Is Black?*

42. See Nicole Isaacson, "The Fetus-Infant: Changing Classifications of *In-Utero* Development in Medical Texts," *Sociological Forum* 11 (1996): 457–480.

43. See, for example, William Beare, *The Roman Stage* (London: Methuen, 1964), 3rd ed., p. 238.

44. See, for example, Zerubavel, *The Fine Line*, pp. 55–57, 106–114.

45. See Simon Dinitz and Nancy Beran, "Community Mental Health as a Boundaryless and Boundary-Busting System," *Journal of Health and Social Behavior* 12 (1971): 99–108.

46. See, for example, Rosabeth M. Kanter, *The Change Masters: Innovations for Productivity in the American Corporation* (New York: Touchstone, 1984).

47. See also Richard M. Merelman, *Making Something of Ourselves: On Culture and Politics in the United States* (Berkeley: University of California Press, 1984), pp. 142–145.

48. Sigfried Giedion, *Space, Time, and Architecture: The Growth of a New Tradition* (Cambridge, Mass.: Harvard University Press, 1956), 3rd ed., pp. 225, 237, 252, 264–268; Vincent J. Scully, *Modern Architecture* (New York: George Braziller, 1974 [1961]), p. 13.

49. See also Oswald Spengler, *The Decline of the West* (New York: Alfred A. Knopf, 1926), vol. 1, pp. 183ff; Frank Lloyd Wright, *The Natural House* (New York: Horizon, 1954), pp. 19–20, 39–40, 45, 50, 137, 165–166; Giedion, *Space, Time, and Architecture*, pp. 398, 543–544; Scully, *Modern Architecture*, pp. 13–21; Zerubavel, *The Fine Line*, pp. 106–107.

50. Ehrenzweig, *The Psychoanalysis of Artistic Vision and Hearing*, p. 23; Giedion, *Space, Time, and Architecture*, pp. 433–434.

51. See, for example, Pirandello, *Tonight We Improvise*, pp. 39–46; Edward E. Cummings, *A Selection of Poems* (New York: Harvest, 1965), p. 140; Michael Kirby (ed.), *Happenings: An Illustrated Anthology* (New

York: E. P. Dutton, 1965); Kaprow, *Assemblage, Environments, and Happenings*, pp. 185–187, 193, 210–341; Zerubavel, *The Fine Line*, p. 108.

52. See also Kaprow, *Assemblage, Environments, and Happenings*, pp. 188–189; Harriet Janis and Rudi Blesh, *Collage* (Philadelphia: Chilton, 1967), pp. 17, 268; Schechner, *Environmental Theater*; pp. 7, 49–53, 59; Zerubavel, *The Fine Line*, pp. 108–110.

53. See, for example, Kirby, *Happenings*, pp. 22, 29; Kaprow, *Assemblage, Environments, and Happenings*, pp. 154–158, 165; Janis and Blesh, *Collage*, pp. 15–24, 55, 60, 88–89, 110–111, 130, 268, 284–288; Zerubavel, *The Fine Line*, pp. 109–110.

54. See, for example, Alexander Frazier, *Open Schools for Children* (Washington, D.C.: Association for Supervision and Curriculum Development, 1972).

55. See, for example, Nena O'Neill and George O'Neill, *Open Marriage: A New Life Style for Couples* (New York: M. Evans, 1972).

56. Clifford Geertz, "Blurred Genres: The Refiguration of Social Thought," in *Local Knowledge: Further Essays in Interpretive Anthropology* (New York: Basic, 1983 [1980]), p. 20.

57. "Have Gays Taken over Yale?" *Newsweek*, October 12, 1987, p. 96.

58. Zerubavel, *Hidden Rhythms*, pp. 147–166; Nippert-Eng, *Home and Work*, pp. 152–193.

59. Zerubavel, *The Fine Line*, pp. 67–70.

60. See, for example, George G. Simpson, *Principles of Animal Taxonomy* (New York: Columbia University Press, 1961), pp. 137–140.

61. Ruth Simpson, "Neither Clear nor Present: The Social Construction of Safety and Danger," *Sociological Forum* 11 (1996): 549–562.

62. See, for example, Roy Wallis (ed.), *On the Margins of Science: The Social Construction of Rejected Knowledge* (Keele: University of Keele [Sociological Review Monograph no. 27], 1979); Thomas F. Gieryn, "Boundary-Work and the Demarcation of Science from Non-Science: Strains and Interests in Professional Ideologies of Scientists," *American Sociological Review* 48 (1983): 781–795; Nachman Ben-Yehuda, *Deviance and Moral Boundaries: Witchcraft, the Occult, Science Fiction, Deviant Sciences and Scientists* (Chicago: University of Chicago Press, 1985), pp. 106–167.

63. See M. Martin Halley and William F. Harvey, "Medical vs. Legal Definitions of Death," *Journal of the American Medical Association* 204 (May 6, 1968): 423–425.

64. Zerubavel, *The Fine Line,* pp. 68–69; Isaacson, "The Fetus-Infant."

65. See also Stephen J. Gould, "Taxonomy as Politics: The Harm of False Classification," *Dissent* (Winter 1990): 73–78; Paul Starr, "Social Categories and Claims in the Liberal State," in Mary Douglas and David Hull (eds.), *How Classification Works: Nelson Goodman among the Social Sciences* (Edinburgh: Edinburgh University Press, 1992), pp. 154–179.

66. Pierre Bourdieu, *Distinction: A Social Critique of the Judgement of Taste* (Cambridge, Mass.: Harvard University Press, 1984 [1979], pp. 479–481.

67. Anaxagoras, quoted in Sven-Tage Teodorsson, *Anaxagoras' Theory of Matter* (Göteborg, Sweden: Acta Universitatis Gothoburgensis, 1982), p. 99.

68. Arthur O. Lovejoy, *The Great Chain of Being: A Study of the History of an Idea* (Cambridge, Mass.: Harvard University Press, 1964 [1936]), p. 56.

69. See also Zerubavel, *Terra Cognita,* pp. 24–29.

70. Ken Wilber, *No Boundary: Eastern and Western Approaches to Personal Growth* (Boston: New Science Library, 1981 [1979]), pp. 24–25. See also C. B. Fawcett, *Frontiers* (Oxford: Oxford University Press, 1918), pp. 17–19, 24.

71. Zerubavel, *The Fine Line,* pp. 9–10, 30–31.

72. See also Peter M. Blau and Otis D. Duncan, *The American Occupational Structure* (New York: Wiley, 1967), p. 124.

73. See, for example, D. L. Rosenhan, "On Being Sane in Insane Places," *Science* 179 (1973): 250–258.

74. Zerubavel, *The Fine Line,* pp. 70–74.

75. Ludwig Wittgenstein, *Philosophical Investigations* (New York: Macmillan, 1958 [1953]), part I, pp. 68–71; Lotfi A. Zadeh, "Fuzzy Sets," *Information and Control* 8 (1965): 338–353; George Lakoff, "Hedges: A Study in Meaning Criteria and the Logic of Fuzzy Concepts," *Journal of Philosophical Logic* 2 (1973): 458–508; Eleanor H. Rosch, "On the Internal Structure of Perceptual and Semantic Categories," in Timothy E. Moore (ed.), *Cognitive Development and the Acquisition of Language* (New York: Academic Press, 1973), pp. 111–144; Michael E. McCloskey and Sam Glucksberg, "Natural Categories: Well Defined or Fuzzy Sets?" *Memory and Cognition* 6 (1978): 462–472; Linda Coleman and Paul Kay, "Prototype Semantics: The English Word *Lie,*" *Language* 57 (1981): 26–44; Zerubavel, *The Fine Line,* pp. 74–80; Taylor, *Linguistic Categorization,* pp. 38–80.

76. See, for example, Kathleen Gerson, *Hard Choices: How Women*

Decide about Work, Career, and Motherhood (Berkeley: University of California Press, 1985); Cynthia F. Epstein, *Deceptive Distinctions: Sex, Gender, and the Social Order* (New Haven: Yale University Press, 1988); Kathleen Gerson, *No Man's Land: Men's Changing Commitments to Family and Work* (New York: Basic Books, 1993).

77. See Whorf, "Science and Linguistics"; Carroll and Casagrande, "The Functions of Language Classifications in Behavior"; Wilber, *No Boundary*, p. 26; Zerubavel, *The Fine Line*, pp. 69–70, 78–79, 84.

78. On mental "lumping," see Zerubavel, "Lumping and Splitting."

79. See also Fred Davis, "Decade Labeling: The Play of Collective Memory and Narrative Plot," *Symbolic Interaction* 7, no. 1 (1984): 15–24.

80. Isaacson, "The Fetus-Infant."

81. See Johanna Foster, "Menstrual Time: The Sociocognitive Mapping of 'the Menstrual Cycle,'" *Sociological Forum* 11 (1996): 533–535.

82. See, for example, Durkheim, *The Elementary Forms of Religious Life*, pp. 433–440; Durkheim, "The Dualism of Human Nature."

83. See also Zerubavel, *The Fine Line*, pp. 28–32.

84. See also Henri Bergson, *Matter and Memory* (London: George Allen & Unwin, 1911 [1908]), pp. 239–298.

85. Nippert-Eng, *Home and Work*, pp. 7–18. See also Zerubavel, "The Rigid, the Fuzzy, and the Flexible."

5. Social Meanings

1. Ferdinand de Saussure, *Course in General Linguistics* (New York: Philosophical Library, 1959 [1915]), p. 67.

2. See also Thorstein Veblen, *The Theory of the Leisure Class: An Economic Study of Institutions* (New York: New American Library, 1953 [1899]).

3. See, for example, Nippert-Eng, *Home and Work*, pp. 50–57.

4. See, for example, Zerubavel, *Hidden Rhythms*, pp. 122–123.

5. See also Gregory Stone, "Appearance and the Self," in Arnold M. Rose (ed.), *Human Behavior and Social Processes* (Boston: Houghton Mifflin, 1962), pp. 86–118; Roland Barthes, *The Fashion System* (New York: Hill and Wang, 1983 [1967]); Sahlins, *Culture and Practical Reason*, pp. 179–196; Fred Davis, *Fashion, Culture, and Identity* (Chicago: University of Chicago Press, 1992).

6. On the "language" of time, see Edward T. Hall, *The Silent Language* (New York: Premier, 1959), pp. 15–21; Eviatar Zerubavel, "The Language of Time: Towards a Semiotics of Temporality," *Sociological Quarterly* 28 (1987): 343–347, 353–354. See also Barry Schwartz, "Waiting, Exchange, and Power: The Distribution of Time in Social Systems," in *Queuing and Waiting: Studies in the Social Organization of Access and Delay* (Chicago: University of Chicago Press, 1975 [1974]), pp. 13–46.

7. This typology is obviously inspired by Charles Peirce's fundamental distinction between "index," "symbol," and "icon." See *Collected Papers of Charles Sanders Peirce,* ed. Charles Hartshorne and Paul Weiss (Cambridge, Mass.: Belknap Press of Harvard University Press, 1962 [1932]), vol. 2, pp. 156–173.

8. Unlike indicative signification (consider, for example, the temporal relation between fire and smoke), iconic representation also does not require any physical juxtaposition between signifiers and what they are supposed to represent to us. No one who regards the cross as representing Christ today, after all, has actually seen the Crucifixion.

9. Susanne K. Langer, *Philosophy in a New Key: A Study in the Symbolism of Reason, Rite, and Art* (Cambridge, Mass.: Harvard University Press, 1942), p. 69.

10. See also Leslie A. White, *The Science of Culture: A Study of Man and Civilization* (New York: Farrar, Straus and Giroux, 1949), pp. 22–39.

11. Edmund Leach, *Culture and Communication: The Logic by which Symbols Are Connected* (Cambridge: Cambridge University Press, 1976), pp. 58–59.

12. Saussure, *Course in General Linguistics,* pp. 115–122. For some classic applications of Saussure's "structuralist" approach to signification, see Roman Jakobson, *Six Lectures on Sound and Meaning* (Cambridge, Mass.: MIT Press, 1978 [1942]); Claude Lévi-Strauss, *The Raw and the Cooked* (New York: Harper and Row, 1969 [1964]). See also Frake, "The Ethnographic Study of Cognitive Systems."

13. See, for example, Pierre Bourdieu, "The Berber House," in Mary Douglas (ed.), *Rules and Meanings: The Anthropology of Everyday Knowledge* (Harmondsworth: Penguin, 1973 [1971]), pp. 98–110; Karen A. Cerulo, "Putting It Together: Measuring the Syntax of Aural and Verbal Symbols," in Robert Wuthnow (ed.), *Vocabularies of Public Life* (London: Routledge, 1992), pp. 111–129; Karen A. Cerulo, *Identity Designs: The*

Sights and Sounds of a Nation (New Brunswick, N.J.: Rutgers University Press, 1995).

14. I first used a "semiotic square" to demonstrate the inseparability of semantics from syntactics in Zerubavel, "The Language of Time," pp. 347–353.

15. Eviatar Zerubavel, *The Seven-Day Circle: The History and Meaning of the Week* (Chicago: University of Chicago Press, 1989 [1985]), pp. 20–23. Consider also, in this regard, the unmistakably anti-Christian symbolism of the calendar of the French Revolution. Ibid., pp. 28–35; Zerubavel, *Hidden Rhythms,* pp. 82–95.

16. Eviatar Zerubavel, "Easter and Passover: On Calendars and Group Identity," *American Sociological Review* 47 (1982): 284–289.

17. For some classic "structuralist" analyses of the "language" of food, see Claude Lévi-Strauss, *The Origin of Table Manners* (New York: Harper and Row, 1978 [1968]), pp. 477–495; Douglas, "Deciphering a Meal," pp. 251–260.

18. See, for example, Brekhus, "Social Marking and the Mental Coloring of Identity." On semiotic markedness, see also Linda R. Waugh, "Marked and Unmarked: A Choice between Unequals in Semiotic Structure," *Semiotica* 38 (1982): 299–318.

19. Zerubavel, *Hidden Rhythms,* p. 145.

20. Zerubavel, *The Seven-Day Circle,* pp. 113–120. On the social marking of time, see also Henri Hubert, "Etude Sommaire de la Représentation du Temps dans la Religion et la Magie," in Henri Hubert and Marcel Mauss (eds.), *Mélanges d'Histoire des Religions* (Paris: Félix Alcan and Guillaumin, 1909 [1905]), pp. 189–229; Edmund Leach, "Two Essays Concerning the Symbolic Representation of Time," in *Rethinking Anthropology* (London: Athlone, 1961), pp. 124–136; Zerubavel, *Patterns of Time in Hospital Life,* pp. 113–123; Foster, "Menstrual Time"; Eviatar Zerubavel, "The Social Marking of Time" (paper presented at the Cultural Turn conference in Santa Barbara, February 1997).

21. See, for example, Hall, *The Hidden Dimension,* pp. 154–164.

22. Raymond Firth, *Symbols: Public and Private* (Ithaca, N.Y.: Cornell University Press, 1973), pp. 272–274, 283.

23. See, for example, Joan P. Emerson, "Behavior in Private Places: Sustaining Definitions of Reality in Gynecological Examinations," in Hans-Peter Dreitzel (ed.), *Recent Sociology No.2: Patterns of Communicative*

Behavior (London: Macmillan, 1970), pp. 74–97. See also Davis, *Smut,* pp. 216–225.

24. See also Durkheim, *The Elementary Forms of Religious Life,* pp. 230–231.

25. See also Durkheim, *The Division of Labor in Society,* pp. 39–41.

26. In a somewhat similar vein, playwright Sam Shepard reminds us in *Fool for Love* (San Francisco: City Lights Books, 1983), only after learning that she might actually be one's half-sister does sleeping with one's lover suddenly become revolting.

27. See Simpson, "Neither Clear Nor Present."

28. See, for example, Durkheim, "The Dualism of Human Nature and Its Social Conditions"; Mead, *Mind, Self, and Society,* pp. 117–125; Berger and Luckmann, *The Social Construction of Reality.* On "semiotic mediation," see also James V. Wertsch, "A Sociocultural Approach to Socially Shared Cognition," in Lauren B. Resnick, John M. Levine, and Stephanie D. Teasley (eds.), *Perspectives on Socially Shared Cognition* (Washington, D.C.: American Psychological Association, 1991), p. 93.

29. See also Durkheim, *The Elementary Forms of Religious Life,* pp. 221–235.

30. See Alfred Korzybski, *Science and Sanity: An Introduction to Non-Aristotelian Systems and General Semantics* (Lakeville, Conn.: International Non-Aristotelian Library Publishing Co., 1958), 4th ed., pp. 58–59, 750–751.

31. Indeed, it is precisely this quality of fetishism that led Marx to use it as a metaphor for the capitalist attachment to commodities. See Karl Marx, *Capital: A Critique of Political Economy* (New York: International Publishers, 1967 [1867]), vol. 1, pp. 71–83.

32. See, for example, George Orwell, "The Principles of Newspeak," in *Nineteen Eighty-Four* (New York: Signet, 1961 [1949]), p. 247. See also Herbert Marcuse, *One-Dimensional Man: Studies in the Ideology of Advanced Industrial Society* (Boston: Beacon, 1964), pp. 85–104.

33. Lewis Carroll, "Through the Looking-Glass," in *The Complete Works of Lewis Carroll* (New York: Vintage, 1976 [1872]), p. 214. See also Whorf, "Language, Mind, and Reality," pp. 259–261.

34. Langer, *Philosophy in a New Key,* p. 75.

35. On the fundamental difference between use and exchange value, see Marx, *Capital,* vol. 1, pp. 35–70.

36. See also White, *The Science of Culture,* p. 29; Norbert Wiener, *The*

Human Use of Human Beings: Cybernetics and Society (Garden City, N.Y.: Doubleday Anchor, 1954), rev. ed., p. 75.

37. Zerubavel, *The Fine Line*, pp. 120–122.

38. On the inverse relations between cognitive rigidity and creativity, see ibid., pp. 116–118.

6. Social Memories

1. See, for example, Ulric Neisser and Eugene Winograd (eds.), *Remembering Reconsidered: Ecological and Traditional Approaches to the Study of Memory* (Cambridge: Cambridge University Press, 1988).

2. See, for example, Maurice Halbwachs, *The Collective Memory* (New York: Harper Colophon, 1980 [1950]), pp. 22–24.

3. See also Maurice Halbwachs, *The Social Frameworks of Memory,* in Lewis A. Coser (ed.), *Maurice Halbwachs on Collective Memory* (Chicago: University of Chicago Press, 1992 [1925]), p. 74.

4. See also Vered Vinitzky-Seroussi, *Looking Forward, Looking Back: High School Reunions and the Social Construction of Identities* (Chicago: University of Chicago Press, forthcoming).

5. See also Steen F. Larsen, "Remembering without Experiencing: Memory for Reported Events," in Ulric Neisser and Eugene Winograd (eds.), *Remembering Reconsidered: Ecological and Traditional Approaches to the Study of Memory* (Cambridge: Cambridge University Press, 1988), p. 337.

6. Zerubavel, "Horizons," pp. 406–408.

7. See also Eviatar Zerubavel, "In the Beginning: Notes on the Social Construction of Historical Discontinuity," *Sociological Inquiry* 63 (1993): 457–459.

8. See also Bernard Lewis, *History: Remembered, Recovered, Invented* (Princeton: Princeton University Press, 1975), pp. 31–32.

9. On sociologists' remarkably short memory, see also Herbert J. Gans, "Sociological Amnesia: The Noncumulation of Normal Social Science," *Sociological Forum* 7 (1992): 701–710.

10. See Gwyn Jones, *The Norse Atlantic Saga* (Oxford: Oxford University Press, 1986), 2nd ed., pp. 144, 156.

11. For some other notable exclusions from that narrative, see Zerubavel, *Terra Cognita*, pp. 36–66, 117–118.

12. Ibid., pp. 22–23.

13. See also Peter L. Berger, *Invitation to Sociology: A Humanistic Perspective* (Garden City, N.Y.: Doubleday Anchor, 1963), pp. 54–65; Peter L. Berger and Hansfried Kellner, "Marriage and the Construction of Reality: An Exercise in the Microsociology of Knowledge," in Hans-Peter Dreitzel (ed.), *Recent Sociology No. 2: Patterns of Communicative Behavior* (London: Macmillan, 1970 [1964]), pp. 62–64.

14. Bartlett, *Remembering*, pp. 254–255.

15. See, for example, Walter Kintsch and Edith Greene, "The Role of Culture-Specific Schemata in the Comprehension and Recall of Stories," *Discourse Processes* 1 (1978): 1–13; Claudia E. Cohen, "Person Categories and Social Perception: Testing Some Boundaries of the Processing Effects of Prior Knowledge," *Journal of Personality and Social Psychology* 40 (1981): 441–452; Fiske and Taylor, *Social Cognition*, pp. 152–153, 161–162; Jean M. Mandler, *Stories, Scripts, and Scenes: Aspects of Schema Theory* (Hillsdale, N.J.: Lawrence Erlbaum, 1984), pp. 93–108; Robert Pritchard, "The Effects of Cultural Schemata on Reading Processing Strategies," *Reading Research Quarterly* 25 (1990): 273–295.

16. Roger C. Schank and Robert P. Abelson, "Scripts, Plans, and Knowledge," in P. N. Johnson-Laird and P. C. Wason (eds.), *Thinking: Readings in Cognitive Science* (Cambridge: Cambridge University Press, 1977), p. 430.

17. Rumelhart and Ortony, "The Representation of Knowledge in Memory," p. 117.

18. Hayden White, "The Historical Text as Literary Artifact," in *Tropics of Discourse: Essays in Cultural Criticism* (Baltimore: Johns Hopkins University Press, 1978 [1974]), pp. 81–99. See also Mandler, *Stories, Scripts, and Scenes*, p. 18; S. Wojciech Sokolowski, "Historical Tradition in the Service of Ideology," *Conjecture* (September 1992): 4–11; Yael Zerubavel, *Recovered Roots: Collective Memory and the Making of Israeli National Tradition* (Chicago: University of Chicago Press, 1995), pp. 216–221.

19. See, for example, Zerubavel, *Recovered Roots*, pp. 17–22.

20. See, for example, Bartlett, *Remembering*; Kintsch and Greene, "The Role of Culture-Specific Schemata in the Comprehension and Recall of Stories"; Margaret S. Steffensen, Chitra Joag-Dev, and Richard C. Anderson, "A Cross-Cultural Perspective on Reading Comprehension," *Reading Research Quarterly* 15 (1979): 10–29; Marjorie Y. Lipson, "The Influence of Religious Affiliation on Children's Memory for Text Information," *Reading*

Research Quarterly 18 (1983): 448–457; Pritchard, "The Effects of Cultural Schemata on Reading Processing Strategies."

21. See, for example, Bartlett, *Remembering*, pp. 249–251; Steffensen, Joag-Dev, and Anderson, "Cross-Cultural Perspective on Reading Comprehension."

22. See also Schutz and Luckmann, *The Structures of the Life-World*, pp. 77, 229–241; Berger and Luckmann, *The Social Construction of Reality*, pp. 30–34; Zerubavel, *The Fine Line*, p. 17.

23. Schutz and Luckmann, *The Structures of the Life-World*.

24. See also, in this regard, Ruth Simpson, "I Was There: Establishing Ownership of Historical Moments" (paper presented at the annual meeting of the American Sociological Association, Los Angeles, August 1994).

25. See also Larsen, "Remembering without Experiencing."

26. See also Barbie Zelizer, *Covering the Body: The Kennedy Assassination, the Media, and the Shaping of Collective Memory* (Chicago: University of Chicago Press, 1992).

27. See also Iwona Irwin-Zarecka, *Frames of Remembrance: The Dynamics of Collective Memory* (New Brunswick, N.J.: Transaction, 1994), p. 47 on "communities of memory."

28. On the traditional Jewish duty to remember one's national past, see also Yosef H. Yerushalmi, *Zakhor: Jewish History and Jewish Memory* (Seattle: University of Washington Press, 1982).

29. I borrow this term from Lisa Bonchek, "Fences and Bridges: The Use of Material Objects in the Social Construction of Continuity and Discontinuity of Time and Identity" (unpublished manuscript, Rutgers University, Department of Sociology, 1994).

30. See also Steven Knapp, "Collective Memory and the Actual Past," *Representations* 26 (1989): 134–147.

31. On the state-sponsored study of national history, see, for example, Frances FitzGerald, *America Revised: History Schoolbooks in the Twentieth Century* (New York: Vintage, 1980); Gilmer W. Blackburn, *Education in the Third Reich: Race and History in Nazi Textbooks* (Albany: State University of New York Press, 1985); Zerubavel, *Recovered Roots*.

32. See Pierre Nora, "Between Memory and History: Les Lieux de Memoire," *Representations* 26 (1989): 7–25.

33. See, for example, Jan Vansina, *Oral Tradition as History* (Madison: University of Wisconsin Press, 1985).

34. See, for example, Zerubavel, *Terra Cognita*, pp. 14–17.

35. See Zerubavel, *Patterns of Time in Hospital Life*, pp. 45–46.

36. See also Georg Simmel, "Written Communication," in Kurt H. Wolff (ed.), *The Sociology of Georg Simmel* (New York: Free Press, 1950 [1908]), pp. 352–355; Weber, *Economy and Society*, pp. 219, 957; M. T. Clanchy, *From Memory to Written Record: England, 1066–1307* (Cambridge, Mass.: Harvard University Press, 1979); Edward Shils, *Tradition* (Chicago: University of Chicago Press, 1981), pp. 109–112, 120–124, 140–147.

37. Shils, *Tradition*, pp. 63–72; David Lowenthal, *The Past Is a Foreign Country* (Cambridge: Cambridge University Press, 1985), pp. 238–249.

38. See, for example, Samuel C. Heilman, *A Walker in Jerusalem* (New York: Summit Books, 1986), pp. 77–111. See also Halbwachs, *The Collective Memory*, pp. 128–136.

39. See, for example, Kevin Lynch, *What Time Is This Place?* (Cambridge, Mass.: MIT Press, 1972), pp. 29–64, 235–238; E. R. Chamberlin, *Preserving the Past* (London: J. M. Dent, 1979); Lowenthal, *The Past Is a Foreign Country*, pp. 384–406.

40. See, for example, Lewis, *History*, pp. 6–7, 33–34, 101; Neil A. Silberman, *Between Past and Present: Archaeology, Ideology, and Nationalism in the Modern Middle East* (New York: Holt, 1989); Zerubavel, *Recovered Roots*, pp. 56–59, 63–68, 129–133, 185–189.

41. See, for example, Daniel J. Sherman, "Art, Commerce, and the Production of Memory in France after World War I," in John R. Gillis (ed.), *Commemorations: The Politics of National Identity* (Princeton: Princeton University Press, 1994), pp. 186–211; James E. Young (ed.), *The Art of Memory: Holocaust Memorials in History* (Munich: Prestel, 1994); Omer Bartov, *Murder in Our Midst: The Holocaust, Industrial Killing, and Representation* (New York: Oxford University Press, 1996), pp. 153–157, 175–186.

42. See also Ira Silver, "Role Transitions, Objects, and Identity," *Symbolic Interaction* (forthcoming).

43. Shils, *Tradition*, pp. 72–74.

44. See Barry Schwartz, "The Social Context of Commemoration: A Study in Collective Memory," *Social Forces* 61 (1982): 374–396.

45. See also Lowenthal, *The Past Is a Foreign Country*, pp. 257–258.

46. Gary Gumpert, *Talking Tombstones and Other Tales of the Media Age* (New York: Oxford University Press, 1987), pp. 56–64. See also Eviatar Zerubavel, "Time and Technology: On the Modern Relations between

Humans and Temporality" (paper presented at the annual meeting of the Social Science History Association, St. Louis, October 1986).

47. This increasingly popular term was first introduced by Maurice Halbwachs in 1925 in *The Social Frameworks of Memory.*

48. See also Vansina, *Oral Tradition as History,* p. 149.

49. Cooley, *Social Organization,* pp. 121–122. See also Durkheim, *The Elementary Forms of Religious Life,* pp. 436–437.

50. See, for example, Yael Zerubavel, "The Death of Memory and the Memory of Death: Masada and the Holocaust as Historical Metaphors," *Representations* 45 (1994): 72–100.

51. On the fundamental difference between the genuinely personal and merely personalized manifestations of the collective, see Durkheim, *The Rules of Sociological Method,* pp. 50–59; Durkheim, *Suicide,* pp. 297–325. See also Zerubavel, *Patterns of Time in Hospital Life,* pp. 106–109.

52. Michael Frisch, "American History and the Structures of Collective Memory: A Modest Exercise in Empirical Iconography," *Journal of American History* 75 (1989): 1130–1155.

53. See Mircea Eliade, *The Sacred and the Profane: The Nature of Religion* (New York: Harcourt, Brace & World, 1959 [1957]), pp. 68–113; Paul Connerton, *How Societies Remember* (Cambridge: Cambridge University Press, 1989), pp. 41–48.

54. Zerubavel, *Hidden Rhythms,* p. 109; Zerubavel, *The Seven-Day Circle,* pp. 20–23.

55. See, for example, David Cressy, *Bonfires and Bells: National Memory and the Protestant Calendar in Elizabethan and Stuart England* (Berkeley: University of California Press, 1989); Zerubavel, *Recovered Roots,* pp. 138–144, 216–221; Eviatar Zerubavel and Yael Zerubavel, "Calendars and National Memory: The Semiotics of History in Modern Israel" (forthcoming).

56. Zerubavel, "Easter and Passover."

57. Zerubavel, *Hidden Rhythms,* pp. 84–88.

58. See, for example, Kirkpatrick Sale, *The Conquest of Paradise: Christopher Columbus and the Columbian Legacy* (New York: Alfred A. Knopf, 1990).

59. See Zerubavel, *Recovered Roots,* pp. 179–185, 200–203.

60. See Michael Schudson, *Watergate in American Memory: How We Remember, Forget, and Reconstruct the Past* (New York: Basic, 1992).

61. See Martin Bernal, *Black Athena: The Afroasiatic Roots of Classical Civilization* (New Brunswick, N.J.: Rutgers University Press, 1987).

62. Zerubavel, *The Fine Line*, pp. 68–69; Zerubavel, "In the Beginning"; Zerubavel, "Horizons," pp. 407–408; Isaacson, "The Fetus-Infant"; Foster, "Menstrual Time."

63. That is also true of "where" it should end. See Zerubavel, *Recovered Roots*, pp. 221–228.

64. See, for example, FitzGerald, *America Revised;* Barry Schwartz, "The Reconstruction of Abraham Lincoln," in David Middleton and Derek Edwards (eds.), *Collective Remembering* (London: Sage, 1990), pp. 81–104; Barry Schwartz, "Social Change and Collective Memory: The Democratization of George Washington," *American Sociological Review* 56 (1991): 221–234; Zerubavel, *Recovered Roots.*

7. Standard Time

1. On temporal reference frameworks, see Zerubavel, *Patterns of Time in Hospital Life*, pp. 84–104; John A. Robinson, "Temporal Reference Systems and Autobiographical Memory," in David C. Rubin (ed.), *Autobiographical Memory* (Cambridge: Cambridge University Press, 1986), pp. 159–188.

2. Kurt Vonnegut, *Cat's Cradle* (New York: Dell, 1970 [1963]), p. 11. See also Lawrence Durrell, *Prospero's Cell: A Guide to the Landscape and Manners of the Island of Corcyra* (London: Faber and Faber, 1945), p. 63.

3. See, for example, Pitirim A. Sorokin and Robert K. Merton, "Social Time: A Methodological and Functional Analysis," *American Journal of Sociology* 42 (1937): 623–624.

4. See also Vansina, *Oral Tradition as History,* p. 175.

5. Zerubavel, *Hidden Rhythms,* p. 97.

6. See, however, Julius A. Roth, *Timetables: Structuring the Passage of Time in Hospital Treatment and Other Careers* (Indianapolis: Bobbs-Merrill, 1963), pp. 30–59; Zerubavel, *Patterns of Time in Hospital Life,* pp. 90–91.

7. See, for example, Alfred Schutz, "Making Music Together: A Study in Social Relationship," *Social Research* 18 (1951): 76–97; Zerubavel, *Patterns of Time in Hospital Life,* pp. 108–109.

8. See, for example, Zerubavel, *Patterns of Time in Hospital Life,* pp. 60–83.

9. See, for example, Amos H. Hawley, *Human Ecology: A Theory of Community Structure* (New York: Ronald Press, 1950), pp. 288–316.

10. Durkheim, *The Elementary Forms of Religious Life,* p. 16. See also Pitirim A. Sorokin, *Sociocultural Causality, Space, Time: A Study of Referential Principles of Sociology and Social Science* (Durham, N.C.: Duke University Press, 1943), p. 173; Radhakamal Mukerjee, "Time, Technics, and Society," *Sociology and Social Research* 27 (1943): 257–258.

11. On the fundamental difference between personal and social time reckoning, see Durkheim, *The Elementary Forms of Religious Life,* p. 10; Schutz and Luckmann, *The Structures of the Life-World,* pp. 27–36.

12. See, for example, Sholem Asch, *Kiddush Ha-Shem* (Tel-Aviv: Dvir, 1953 [1919]), p. 13.

13. Berger and Luckmann, *The Social Construction of Reality,* p. 28. See also Zerubavel, *The Seven-Day Circle,* pp. 2–3.

14. See, for example, Daniel Defoe, *The Life and Strange Surprising Adventures of Robinson Crusoe, Mariner* (London: Oxford University Press, 1972 [1719]), p. 64. See also Dalton Trumbo, *Johnny Got His Gun* (New York: Bantam, 1970 [1939]), pp. 126–143.

15. Leo Tolstoy, "The Death of Ivan Ilych," in *The Death of Ivan Ilych and Other Stories* (New York: Signet Classics, 1960 [1886]), p. 139.

16. See, for example, Zerubavel, *The Seven-Day Circle,* p. 137.

17. See also David S. Landes, *Revolution in Time: Clocks and the Making of the Modern World* (Cambridge, Mass.: Harvard University Press, 1983), pp. 85–89.

18. See also Georg Simmel, "The Metropolis and Mental Life," in Kurt H. Wolff (ed.), *The Sociology of Georg Simmel* (New York: Free Press, 1950 [1903]), pp. 412–413.

19. On how it came to be a global system, see Derek Howse, *Greenwich Time and the Discovery of the Longitude* (Oxford: Oxford University Press, 1980), pp. 116–171; Zerubavel, *Hidden Rhythms,* pp. 96–100; Eviatar Zerubavel, "The Standardization of Time: A Sociohistorical Perspective," *American Journal of Sociology* 88 (1982): 12–17; Zerubavel, *The Seven-Day Circle,* pp. 19–26.

20. On the fundamental difference between sociotemporal and physio-

temporal or biotemporal arrangements, see Zerubavel, *Hidden Rhythms,* pp. 1–12, 40–44.

21. On the invention of the standard time-zone system, see Howse, *Greenwich Time and the Discovery of the Longitude,* pp. 121–126; Zerubavel, "The Standardization of Time," pp. 8–15.

22. See, for example, *Today's World: A New World Atlas from the Cartographers of Rand McNally* (Chicago: Rand McNally, 1994), rev. ed., p. viii.

23. See ibid.

24. Indeed, in marked contrast to the numerous clues it offers those who wish to reckon the time of the day (such as the position of the sun in the sky) or year (such as the temperature), nature offers absolutely no clues whatsoever to those who have lost count of the days of the week. Thus, while it is most unlikely that anyone would ever mistake midnight for noon or summer for winter, it is quite possible for someone to actually mistake a Tuesday for a Saturday. See Zerubavel, *The Seven-Day Circle,* pp. 134–138.

25. On the mathematical "harmonics" of social time reckoning, see also ibid., pp. 60–82.

26. Note, in this regard, that even within a single society such as the United States the year officially begins not only on January 1 but also on July 1 (in many hospitals and businesses) as well as around early February (in Chinatowns) and Labor Day (in most schools). By the same token, the day begins not only at midnight but also at 4:00 A.M. (on some train schedules), 6:00 A.M. (in many television listings), and sunset (for Orthodox Jews). See also Zerubavel, *Patterns of Time in Hospital Life,* pp. 8–9, 31–32, 96–97.

27. Indeed, note the considerable initial resistance to the introduction of Greenwich time, the standard time-zone system, or daylight saving time. See, for example, Stewart H. Holbrook, *The Story of American Railroads* (New York: Crown, 1947), pp. 356–359; Howse, *Greenwich Time and the Discovery of the Longitude,* pp. 106–113; Siamak Movahedi, "Cultural Preconcpetions of Time: Can We Use Operational Time to Meddle in God's Time?" *Comparative Studies in Society and History* 27 (1985): 385–400.

28. See Zerubavel, *Hidden Rhythms,* pp. 98–100; Frank Parise (ed.), *The Book of Calendars* (New York: Facts on File, 1982), pp. 295–297.

29. See, for example, Zerubavel, *The Seven-Day Circle,* pp. 27–43, 45–46, 50–54.

30. See Howse, *Greenwich Time and the Discovery of the Longitude,* pp. 160–162. See also Zerubavel, "The Standardization of Time," pp. 15–16.

31. Jules Verne, *Around the World in Eighty Days* (New York: Charles Scribner's Sons, 1906 [1873]).

32. See Howse, *Greenwich Time and the Discovery of the Longitude,* pp. 82–115; Zerubavel, "The Standardization of Time," pp. 5–11.

33. See, for example, John Horton, "Time and Cool People," *Trans-Action* 4, no. 5 (1967), pp. 8–10; Harry Murray, "Time in the Streets," *Human Organization* 43 (1984): 154–161; Zerubavel, *The Seven-Day Circle,* pp. 136–138.

8. Conclusion

1. By contrast, for a discussion of what cognitive science has to offer sociology, see Paul DiMaggio, "Culture and Cognition: An Interdisciplinary Review," *Annual Review of Sociology* (forthcoming).

/ Further Reading

General

Augoustinos, Martha, and John M. Innes. "Towards an Integration of Social Representations and Social Schema Theory." *British Journal of Social Psychology* 29 (1990): 213–231.

Berry, John W., et al. *Cross-Cultural Psychology: Research and Applications.* Cambridge: Cambridge University Press, 1992.

Cole, Michael, and Sylvia Scribner. *Culture and Thought: A Psychological Introduction.* New York: John Wiley, 1974.

DiMaggio, Paul. "Culture and Cognition: An Interdisciplinary Review." *Annual Review of Sociology* (forthcoming).

Farr, Robert M., and Serge Moscovici, eds. *Social Representations.* Cambridge: Cambridge University Press, 1982.

Jahoda, Gustav. *Crossroads between Culture and Mind: Continuities and Change in Theories of Human Nature.* Cambridge, Mass.: Harvard University Press, 1993.

Rogoff, Barbara. *Apprenticeship in Thinking: Cognitive Development in Social Context.* New York: Oxford University Press, 1990.

Wertsch, James V., ed. *Culture, Communication, and Cognition: Vygotskian Perspectives.* Cambridge: Cambridge University Press, 1985.

The Sociology of the Mind

Berger, Peter L., and Thomas Luckmann. *The Social Construction of Reality: A Treatise in the Sociology of Knowledge.* Garden City, N.Y.: Doubleday Anchor, 1967 (1966).

Cole, Michael, and Barbara Means. *Comparative Studies of How People Think: An Introduction.* Cambridge, Mass.: Harvard University Press, 1981.

Davis, Murray S. *Smut: Erotic Reality/Obscene Ideology.* Chicago: University of Chicago Press, 1983.

Durkheim, Emile. "The Dualism of Human Nature and Its Social Conditions." In Robert N. Bellah, ed., *Emile Durkheim: On Morality and Society.* Chicago: University of Chicago Press, 1973 (1914), pp. 149–163.

———— *The Elementary Forms of Religious Life.* New York: Free Press, 1995 (1912).

Fleck, Ludwik. *Genesis and Development of A Scientific Fact.* Chicago: University of Chicago Press, 1979 (1935).

Luria, Alexander, R. *Cognitive Development: Its Cultural and Social Foundations.* Cambridge, Mass.: Harvard University Press, 1976 (1974).

Mannheim, Karl. *Ideology and Utopia: An Introduction to the Sociology of Knowledge.* New York: Harvest, 1936 (1929).

Mead, George H. *Mind, Self, and Society: From the Standpoint of a Social Behaviorist.* Chicago: University of Chicago Press, 1934.

Resnick, Lauren B., John M. Levine, and Stephanie D. Teasley, eds. *Perspectives on Socially Shared Cognition.* Washington, D.C.: American Psychological Association, 1991.

Schutz, Alfred, and Thomas Luckmann. *The Structures of the Life-World.* Evanston, Ill.: Northwestern University Press, 1973.

Social Optics

Berry, John W. "Ecological and Cultural Factors in Spatial Perceptual Development." *Canadian Journal of Behavioural Science* 3 (1971): 324–336.

Laqueur, Thomas. *Making Sex: Body and Gender from the Greeks to Freud.* Cambridge, Mass.: Harvard University Press, 1990.

Reynolds, Ralph E., et al. "Cultural Schemata and Reading Comprehension." *Reading Research Quarterly* 17 (1982): 353–366.

Segall, Marshall H., Donald T. Campbell, and Melville J. Herskovits. *The Influence of Culture on Visual Perception.* Indianapolis: Bobbs-Merrill, 1966.

Shibutani, Tamotsu. "Reference Groups as Perspectives." *American Journal of Sociology* 60 (1955): 562–569.

Simmel, Georg. "The Field of Sociology." In Kurt H. Wolff, ed., *The Sociology of Georg Simmel.* New York: Free Press, 1950 (1917), pp. 3–25.

Zerubavel, Eviatar. *Terra Cognita: The Mental Discovery of America.* New Brunswick, N.J.: Rutgers University Press, 1992.

The Social Gates of Consciousness

Bateson, Gregory. "A Theory of Play and Fantasy." In *Steps to an Ecology of Mind.* New York: Ballantine, 1972 (1955), pp. 177–193.

Emerson, Joan P. "Behavior in Private Places: Sustaining Definitions of Reality in Gynecological Examinations." In Hans-Peter Dreitzel, ed., *Recent Sociology No.2: Patterns of Communicative Behavior.* London: Macmillan, 1970, pp. 74–97.

Goffman, Erving. *Behavior in Public Places: Notes on the Social Organization of Gatherings.* New York: Free Press, 1963.

——— *Frame Analysis: An Essay on the Organization of Experience.* New York: Harper Colophon, 1974.

Kuhn, Thomas S. *The Structure of Scientific Revolutions.* Chicago: University of Chicago Press, 1962.

Purcell, Kristen. "In A League of Their Own: Mental Leveling and the Creation of Social Comparability in Sport." *Sociological Forum* 11 (1996): 435–456.

Rothbart, Myron, Mark Evans, and Solomon Fulero. "Recall for Confirming Events: Memory Processes and the Maintenance of Social Stereotypes." *Journal of Experimental Social Psychology* 15 (1979): 343–355.

Simmel, Georg. "Sociability: An Example of Pure, or Formal Sociology." In Kurt H. Wolff, ed., *The Sociology of Georg Simmel.* New York: Free Press, 1950 (1917), pp. 40–57.

The Social Division of the World

Davis, F. James. *Who Is Black?: One Nation's Definition.* University Park, Penn: Pennsylvania State University Press, 1991.

Douglas, Mary. "Self Evidence." In *Implicit Meanings: Essays in Anthropology.* London: Routledge and Kegan Paul, 1978 (1975), pp. 276–318.

Frake, Charles O. "The Ethnographic Study of Cognitive Systems." In Stephen A. Tyler, ed., *Cognitive Anthropology.* New York: Holt, Rinehart, and Winston, 1969 (1962), pp. 28–41.

Lévi-Strauss, Claude. *The Savage Mind.* Chicago: University of Chicago Press, 1966 (1962).

Starr, Paul. "Social Categories and Claims in the Liberal State." In Mary Douglas and David Hull, eds., *How Classification Works: Nelson Goodman among the Social Sciences.* Edinburgh: Edinburgh University Press, 1992, pp. 154–179.

Whorf, Benjamin L. *Language, Thought, and Reality.* Cambridge, Mass.: MIT Press, 1956.

Zerubavel, Eviatar. *The Fine Line: Making Distinctions in Everyday Life.* Chicago: University of Chicago Press, 1993 (1991).

———— "The Rigid, the Fuzzy, and the Flexible: Notes on the Mental Sculpting of Academic Identity." *Social Research* 62 (1995): 1093–1106.

————, ed. Special Issue: "Lumping and Splitting." *Sociological Forum* 11 (1996): 421–584.

Social Meanings

Barthes, Roland. *Elements of Semiology.* New York: Hill and Wang, 1968 (1964).

Bourdieu, Pierre. "The Berber House." In Mary Douglas, ed., *Rules and Meanings: The Anthropology of Everyday Knowledge.* Harmondsworth: Penguin, 1973 (1971), pp. 98–110.

Brekhus, Wayne. "Social Marking and the Mental Coloring of Identity: Sexual Identity Construction and Maintenance in the United States." *Sociological Forum* 11 (1996): 497–522.

Cerulo, Karen A. *Identity Designs: The Sights and Sounds of a Nation.* New Brunswick, N.J.: Rutgers University Press, 1995.

Hertz, Robert. "The Pre-eminence of the Right Hand: A Study in Religious Polarity." In Rodney Needham, ed., *Right and Left: Essays on Dual Symbolic Classification.* Chicago: University of Chicago Press, 1978 (1909), pp. 3–22.

Leach, Edmund. "Anthropological Aspects of Language: Animal Categories and Verbal Abuse." In Eric H. Lenneberg, ed., *New Directions in the Study of Language.* Cambridge, Mass.: MIT Press, 1964, pp. 23–63.

———— *Culture and Communication: The Logic by Which Symbols Are Connected.* Cambridge: Cambridge University Press, 1976.

Nippert-Eng, Christena. *Home and Work: Negotiating Boundaries through Everyday Life.* Chicago: University of Chicago Press, 1996.

Sahlins, Marshall. *Culture and Practical Reason.* Chicago: University of Chicago Press, 1976.

Schwartz, Barry. *Vertical Classification: A Study in Structuralism and the Sociology of Knowledge.* Chicago: University of Chicago Press, 1981.

Zelizer, Viviana A. *The Social Meaning of Money: Pin Money, Paychecks, Poor Relief, and Other Currencies.* New York: Basic Books, 1994.

Zerubavel, Eviatar. *Hidden Rhythms: Schedules and Calendars in Social Life.* Berkeley: University of California Press, 1985 (1981).

Social Memories

Bartlett, Frederic C. *Remembering: A Study in Experimental and Social Psychology.* Cambridge: Cambridge University Press, 1932.

Coser, Lewis A., ed. *Maurice Halbwachs on Collective Memory.* Chicago: University of Chicago Press, 1992.

FitzGerald, Frances. *America Revised: History Schoolbooks in the Twentieth Century.* New York: Vintage, 1980.

Frisch, Michael. "American History and the Structures of Collective Memory: A Modest Exercise in Empirical Iconography." *Journal of American History* 75 (1989): 1130–1155.

Halbwachs, Maurice. *The Collective Memory.* New York: Harper Colophon, 1980 (1950).

Kintsch, Walter, and Edith Greene. "The Role of Culture-Specific Schemata in the Comprehension and Recall of Stories." *Discourse Processes* 1 (1978): 1–13.

Lewis, Bernard. *History: Remembered, Recovered, Invented.* Princeton: Princeton University Press, 1975.

Schwartz, Barry. "The Social Context of Commemoration: A Study in Collective Memory." *Social Forces* 61 (1982): 374–396.

Zerubavel, Eviatar. "Easter and Passover: On Calendars and Group Identity." *American Sociological Review* 47 (1982): 284–289.

Zerubavel, Yael. *Recovered Roots: Collective Memory and the Making of Israeli National Tradition.* Chicago: University of Chicago Press, 1995.

Standard Time

Roth, Julius A. *Timetables: Structuring the Passage of Time in Hospital Treatment and Other Careers.* Indianapolis: Bobbs-Merrill, 1963.

Sorokin, Pitirim A. *Sociocultural Causality, Space, Time: A Study of Referential Principles of Sociology and Social Science.* Durham, N.C.: Duke University Press, 1943.

Zerubavel, Eviatar. *Patterns of Time in Hospital Life: A Sociological Perspective.* Chicago: University of Chicago Press, 1979.

———— *The Seven-Day Circle: The History and Meaning of the Week.* Chicago: University of Chicago Press, 1989 (1985).

———— "The Standardization of Time: A Sociohistorical Perspective," *American Journal of Sociology* 88 (1982): 1–23.

/ Author Index

/ Subject Index